FOOTBALL
RAISE YOUR
MENTAL GAME

*To Mum for always believing in me,
to Dad for always supporting me when times
were tough. To Michael, David and James, the
best brothers ever, for always being there. And to
Joanne for everything you've done for me.*

FOOTBALL
RAISE YOUR
MENTAL GAME

RICHARD NUGENT AND STEVE BROWN

First published 2008 by
A&C Black Publishers Ltd
38 Soho Square, London W1D 3HB
www.acblack.com

ISBN 978-0-713-68879-5

A CIP catalogue record for this book
is available from the British Library.

Typeset in Galliard by seagulls.net

Cover image © Corbis
Inside photography © PA Photos,
except pages 14, 19, 25, 29 and 139 © iStock

Printed and bound by Caligraving Ltd., Thetford, Norfolk

This book is produced using paper that is made from wood
grown in managed, sustainable forests. It is natural, renewable
and recyclable. The logging and manufacturing processes conform
to the environmental regulations of the country of origin.

CONTENTS

ACKNOWLEDGEMENTS

So much for this being the easy part to write. There are so many people I'd like to thank – apologies if I miss anyone.

The idea for the book came from a coaching session with my talented, beautiful wife Joanne – thank you.

Next to influence the process was Larry Reynolds, whose coaching and support really moved the idea into reality. My huge thanks to Steve Marriott, Alastair Olby, Trevor Durnford, Margaret Ginnelly and especially my guru Kimberley Hare at Kaizen Training. You are the most dynamic, talented and supportive people anyone could ever wish for. Kim, thanks for helping me build the life I want to lead and for giving permission to adapt several of your tools and techniques for the book.

Thank you to Kevin Cherry and Bernadette Doyle. Your coaching was key in the development of Success In Football Ltd and to Michael Neill, simply the greatest coach I've ever learned from. My first two football clients were also great advisors so thanks to Paul McHugh and Craig Armstrong, both of whom are featured in this book. I'm hugely grateful, too, to the other contributors, David Platt of Liverpool, Ralf Wright, Colin Chesters of San Diego Surf and Steve Cook of NC United, whose friendship and energy make my trips to the US valuable, interesting and fun; and James O'Connor, not just a client but also a good friend – you've helped me every bit as much as I have you.

To Shaun, Ryan and Bruce Jobson of Trident Soccer, great coaches and good friends who made the first trip to the US happen and put me in touch with Steve Cook. My appreciation to everyone at Cullercoats FC and Formica FC for listening to these stories over and over, especially Ken Ellis, Lance

Thompson, Len Renham, Ian Booth and the best manager I ever played for – John Wall.

The friends who've been with me along the way could fill three pages so thanks to all the lads, especially Paul Ponton, Ross Aitken, Ian Booth, Daniel Nelson, Andy Bowman, Danny Ponton, Paul Hart, John McCabe, Peter Bradley, Stephen Dynes, Joe Elliott, Andy McColl and James Leggett who I talked this stuff through with.

Special thanks to Steven Hart, Daniel Salmon and my co-author Steve Brown, all people who have been there at the best and worst of times. A big thanks to Darren Long and everyone at Beswicks Sports Lawyers. If Carlsberg did agents they would probably be you. To Maureen and George Bush and David, Gill and Lucy Wilkinson for encouragement and support.

Finally thanks to Charlotte Atyeo and Alex Hazle of A&C Black, along with Robert Foss and Charlotte Croft for developing and supporting this idea and to everyone who helped get this book in front of you.

Richard Nugent

Big, big thanks to Fay and Ken, without whom, nowt. Seriously, I will never, ever, repay you. So stop counting ...

Otherwise, family-wise, Neil and Lou: love you loads. J&D too. To Rich, for the opportunity and the faith.

As for the 'career', I have been putty in the good hands of Martin Hardy, Dylon Younger, Neil Farrington and Stuart Jamieson. And grateful for being shaped so.

And finally, Alan Cutting, who distilled in me the two most important foundations of journalism: rat-like cunning and a taste for Guinness.

Steve Brown

FOREWORD

When I was 19, some friends from university and I played in a football match in Shanghai. What had started out as a casual challenge from some of the locals nearly became an international incident, as over 500 people showed up to watch what we had all thought would be a friendly pick-up game. Despite this, or perhaps because of it, we managed to hold our own against a team that turned out to include an Olympic team member and two other top-level Chinese athletes. What fascinated me then and intrigues me to this day is *how* that was possible. In other words, what happened inside our heads that day which allowed a group of amateurs to play so far beyond our natural ability that a potentially hostile crowd actually applauded us as we came off the pitch?

In this well-written, simple-to-follow book, Richard Nugent and Steve Brown answer that question by teaching the mental side of the game – the difference between good and great; between excellent and world-class. Because of my background as a coach and trainer of Neuro-Linguistic Programming, I was already familiar with many of the practical techniques the authors share for taking your game (or your players' game) to the next level. But what they have done by breaking each technique down into step-by-step exercises is to make these complex psychological techniques simple to understand and easily applicable to nearly any sporting situation.

The other thing that shines through is the authors' passion for excellence and love of the game. If football is your passion you will find yourself among friends in this book.

Whether you are looking for the final piece of the puzzle to excel in the Premier League, for techniques to improve your game at club level or just to set your kids off in the right direction as they begin playing with their friends in the park, you are about to embark on a journey of discovery that will take you far beyond what you currently think is possible.

Michael Neill, bestselling author of *Feel Happy Now* and *You Can Have What You Want*

The mental state of any sportsperson is an essential part of attaining consistency and success. Most football clubs rely on their own versions of mentally preparing the players to deal with all the positives, and indeed negatives, that are part of everyday life as a footballer. Some clubs have employed dedicated sports psychologists while others rely on the 'man management' skills of the coach.

There are some obvious examples of tremendous football managers who can motivate their players throughout a season, year in, year out, but this shouldn't overshadow the situations where specific expertise and outside help could prove vital.

Support for players through what is a psychologically tough profession, both on and off the pitch, could lessen the burden on individuals throughout all the stages of their career.

During my 18 years as a professional footballer, my mental state swung from high to low, confidence to insecurity – I can't think of a time when everything was just simply 'OK'. I had to deal with this myself and, like many players, learned to cope. At times this was a solitary and challenging experience.

Over recent years, almost every aspect of football as a profession has been improved to help teams be more successful and give them an extra edge. However, training players' minds, in many cases, is the sole responsibility of the individual, and while every player has to have an inner strength and a will to succeed, understanding how to deal with the mental pressures would help even the most experienced of players.

I can think of many players who have been technically inferior to their peers but, because of their attitude, desire and mental determination, they succeeded in getting the most out of their ability in contrast to naturally gifted footballers who drifted and underachieved because they didn't – or couldn't – focus their minds.

As a footballer, you have to make the most of what is a very short career. While technical and physical ability is imperative, being mentally prepared will give the individual a far greater chance to succeed.

This book helps demystify aspects of sports psychology and offers practical and straightforward advice to help both players and coaches deal with specific situations. Were I playing now, I have no doubt this book would be a vital reference to me along the way.

Graeme Le Saux, former Chelsea, Blackburn,
Southampton and England defender

INTRODUCTION

GETTING UP FOR A PLAY-OFF GAME — A TRUE-LIFE EXAMPLE OF RAISING YOUR MENTAL GAME

A player who was preparing for a play-off final at the Millennium Stadium rang asking for advice. This player was known for being enthusiastic and he never had any problems getting motivated for games. Yet hours before the biggest game he'd played in since his move out of the Premiership a couple of years before, he was describing how he felt 'flat' and not ready to play.

I asked him why this was such a big game for him. His answer was all about his friends and family, in particular his daughter, watching him playing at the Millennium Stadium.

I asked him to imagine walking out of the tunnel, turning and looking into the stands and catching the eye of his partner and daughter. I asked him to describe what he thought they'd be thinking and feeling. As he did that, I could hear his voice becoming more excited and his breathing getting faster (a clear sign of increased excitement). I then asked him to imagine the feeling of picking his daughter up after winning the game and putting the winners' medal around her neck. He became more and more animated until finally he said he couldn't wait to get on the pitch and get going. In the space of ten minutes, he'd gone from 'flat' and 'not ready' to excited, motivated and ready to go.

So the brain's inability to see the difference between what we imagine and what is 'real' can really help us. As we think about these really positive things, the brain makes us react as if they are happening for real.

This is just one small example of how the tools and techniques we describe in this book have been applied in big games with top professionals. We hope you use them to develop and improve your career, whatever level you play at.

GETTING STARTED

Welcome, and congratulations. By simply picking up this book you've already taken more steps towards developing your mental fitness than most players and coaches, even those at the top level, ever do. But before we go any further, let us ask you a question. How big is the gap between success and failure? A few years ago I attended a seminar led by former England rugby player and now the RFU's Director of Elite Rugby, Rob Andrew. He showed that the gap is just a few seconds. Anthony Robbins, a renowned performance coach from the United States echoes this, describing 'excellent and outstanding' as being only millimetres apart.

The effect on results is, of course, huge. That tiny variation in performance can be the difference not just between winning and losing, but between promotion and relegation, even between getting a contract and being released. Today, when high impact fitness and nutrition programmes are available to the masses and players at all levels and of all ages are receiving a higher standard of coaching than ever before, the differences between players and teams in technical, tactical and physical aspects of the game are reducing. This is why psychological development or mental fitness of players has become increasingly important.

This book has three aims:

- To demystify elements of 'sports psychology'.
- To make tools and techniques for mental fitness readily available to players and coaches at all levels by simplifying the seemingly complicated.
- To make *you* more successful.

The tools and techniques we discuss have been around for a number of years and variations of them have been applied in a number of sports as well as in business. Although they've generally been neglected in football, they have been used with players and coaches from the Premiership through to grassroots football – and that's one of the real bonuses: they are inclusive. As long as you are serious about improving, willing to give them a go and stick with them they have the potential to make a massive difference to you, no matter what level you play or coach at.

The book is in three distinct parts. The first section is written as a toolkit, designed to enable you to 'dip into' a chapter and make improvements in a specific area. If your particular problem isn't described in one of the chapter headings, feel free to choose one that is similar – you're likely to be able to use the same tools to deal with your problem.

The second part of the book 'puts the meat on the bones' of the techniques included in the first chapters. We've done our best to avoid making it too technical or theoretical, while still satisfying those readers who like the 'how' and 'why' before using new approaches. If you're not into the theory, you don't have to read this section – just keep following the instructions in the first part of the book.

The third part is written for managers, coaches and captains. It brings together the latest thinking on how to get the best performance from people by leading rather than just managing, with our experience of working in this field with clubs and managers.

'It only works' – Jack Black, former Performance Coach to Dundee United and Founder of 'Mind Store'

We occasionally get asked who these tools and techniques don't work for. The answer is simple. They definitely don't work for anyone who doesn't use them. Moreover, if you wanted to develop a new technique that you'd seen work for another player or team, would you go on the training pitch and try it once before giving it up as 'not working'? Of course not. Anything new needs to be played with and practised (I don't like the phrase 'working at it' as this implies it'll be hard). The same applies to mental fitness. Many of the exercises will come naturally; others will have to be rehearsed until they become part of your routine.

THE FOUNDATIONS

Many of the exercises, tools and techniques in this book are based on the principle that the body and brain are all one system. In other words, what you think will automatically have an impact on how you feel and what you do.

Here's another way that we can show this:

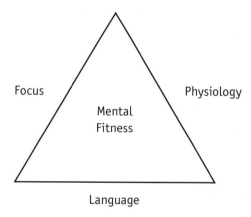

Our mental fitness is a triangle and, in order for us to perform at our best, we must pay attention to each side and ensure that they are balanced.

So what are these three sides?

Focus

Simply put, focus is what we're thinking about. Or, more accurately, what we're *really* thinking about. In football we hear the word 'focus' used quite regularly and often incorrectly. We hear players, managers and commentators talking about 'being focused'. Well here is the news: *we are always focused; what we need to do is focus on the right things.* When a player is about to come out of the dressing room before a cup final, I can guarantee he or she will be focused. What counts is whether they are focusing on all the things they are going to do well or on how stressed they are feeling and how let down the fans are going to be if they play badly.

Physiology

This will be more familiar to many of you. For the purposes of this book we'll label physiology as anything to do with movement and how the body is 'held'. In other words, if you are sitting now, change your body position and sit the way you would if the next chapter of this book was going to change your life forever. Sit the way you would if you were the most interested, most intrigued that you've ever been in all of your life.

If you moved, you've just changed your physiology. If you stood up now and ran around the room, you have changed it again. Whenever you change your physiology your body needs a different mix of 'chemicals' to support the movement (more on that later).

Language

Hopefully you won't need too much explanation as to what language is, but there are some specific distinctions we'd like to make for the purposes of this book.

We're not going to make a judgement on what language is good and what is bad. But what we are going to define clearly is helpful and unhelpful language. We can communicate lots of messages in a way that increases our chances of success or in a way that increases our chances of disappointment.

We'll also make suggestions about changing your language patterns, and detail some words and phrases that may be more helpful to use. We'll give you the reasons behind this and then encourage you to come up with your own ideas. This isn't about creating scripts for you to use. Finally, whatever you read in this book about external language applies to internal language (more about these later in the book).

MENTAL FITNESS

Each of these sides of the triangle impact on each other. For example, your physical fitness (as one aspect of physiology) will impact on the things you say to yourself and how you think you'll perform. Alternatively, if you are being strongly criticised (language), that will have an impact on how your body feels and again change what you think about (playing harder, slapping the 'critic', getting off the pitch as soon as possible and so on).

To give yourself the greatest chance of success, we'd encourage you to implement tools, techniques and strategies that ensure that every aspect of your mental fitness is as well cared for as your physical fitness.

Just How Important Is Mental Fitness?

In several of the clubs we work in, 'psychological development' is set alongside the tactical, technical and physical development of young players, with each area in their development plan being reviewed every few months. This indicates that mental fitness is at least as important as, for example, practising set pieces or developing a tailored fitness programme.

How long do you spend on psychological development at your club?
Here's another indicator of the importance of mental fitness.
How many 'superstars' in sport would you say are mentally
weak? No, we can't think of any either. Anyone who has
achieved, from David Beckham to Muhammad Ali, from Dame
Kelly Holmes to Jose Mourinho, had clear focus (on the right
things) and developed the abilities to deliver their dreams. The
mental fitness came first. We've yet to meet a player who said
'I just realised I could score thirty goals a season' or 'all of a
sudden I was playing for my national team'.

WHAT ELSE DO I NEED TO KNOW?

Everyone is unique

Mental fitness is different in everyone. How one player reacts
to criticism will be different to another player's reaction. That's
what makes it so interesting. This book won't cure everything
for everyone, but what we've aimed to do is provide enough
tools to make a difference to most people and give you enough
information to develop your own strategies too. For coaching
tailored specifically to you, think about engaging your own
performance coach.

Mental Fitness Is Not About 'Fixing The Broken'

One of our pet irritations is that mental coaching is seen as
remedial. We hear from players when they aren't performing
well or clubs contact us when they are relegated. An agent gets
in touch when they discover their client is an addict of some

kind. Of course we can make a huge difference in these circumstances, but how much better would it be for everyone involved to work on mental fitness to prevent any of these circumstances occurring in the first place?

As a player or coach, your knowledge of these tools and techniques will increase your chances of success over the long term. So use it as a development tool, rather than waiting until you need help.

It's written for you

Whether you are a coach or player, and whichever level you're at, so long as you are serious about your football, this book is for you. If an exercise is written for a player and you are a coach, just familiarise yourself with it and then you can apply it.

Another aspect that makes this whole area interesting is that the same strategies work for professionals and grass-roots players (see an example from our experience in the box below).

'I remember one incident when I was helping out a friend by preparing his local Under-19 team for a league play-off. When the session was over, I switched on my phone and I had a message from a professional who was playing in the League Two play-off final the next day at the Millennium Stadium in Cardiff. The tools that I used to help him prepare mentally for that game were almost identical to the tools that I introduced to the U19 team just minutes before. Both teams won, by the way.' Richard

The examples we have given mainly relate to adult men's football just because that is where most of our clients are. However, the tools are just as applicable to everyone else, regardless of their age, gender or ability.

Read and re-read

We think you'll get the most benefit from reading the book through *and* using it as a toolkit. Whichever way around you do it, we'd recommend that you revisit the material over and over. Every time you read it, you'll get a new insight, strategy or idea.

Share it with your team

Football is one of the most 'closed' environments we've come across in terms of sharing ideas, and we can see why. The line between success and failure is so small that people don't like to put their necks on the line. The reality, however, is that the more people in your team and club who know about this stuff the more likely you are to be successful. Even if you leave a club, your legacy will live on and your reputation will continue to grow.

SOME RESEARCH AND STUDIES

We've not met many football people who are 'into' scientific research, so here are some genuine stories that give even more of a flavour of why mental fitness is important.

In 1980 the Soviet Union were preparing for the Winter Olympics. Their athletes were given one of four training programmes. The first concentrated wholly on physical training; the second on 75 per cent physical and 25 per cent mental training; the third on 25 per cent physical and 75 per cent mental training; and the fourth group's training was a 50:50 split.

The group that made the most progress was the group that spent the most time on mental fitness.

Seventy-two basketball players from eight teams took part in a study in 1977 at Hunter College in America. One group began each day with a mental rehearsal of their 'free throw' technique. Coaches reported a 7 per cent increase in the accuracy of this group's shooting. During this research, the players were fitted with sensors that showed that their muscles experienced the same activity during the mental rehearsal as when they actually took the free throws.

Golfers took part in a similar study at the Olympic Research Centre in America, this time with one group visualising a successful putt, a second visualising an unsuccessful putt and the third not visualising at all. The study lasted a week and by the end the group who had used mental rehearsal had improved their putting by 30 per cent. The group that did not use visualisation also improved, but only by 11 per cent. What is most interesting is that the group focusing on negative visualisation reduced their accuracy by a massive 21 per cent. Remember: it's not just about focus; it's about focus on the right things.

These are just a few examples of mental fitness at work: there are many others. If you read any biography of a successful professional footballer, you will get a feel of the importance they place on the mental side of the game and how they have sabotaged themselves during their career by neglecting it.

All of this highlights two major factors about mental fitness:

- Outstanding coaches and players use these techniques naturally. The secret is to understand them and use them more widely.
- It only works. We've never had a client who has used the tools effectively and experienced anything other than success.

As the gap closes in the physical, technical and tactical areas of the game, mental fitness will become the differentiating factor in success. In fact, it already is.

PART 1: COMMON PROBLEMS

CHAPTER 1
I'VE LOST MY CONFIDENCE

Confidence in your own abilities is just a state of mind

There is a secret to confidence that most people don't realise. When you discover it, it can increase your performance, improve communication and help you to become more consistent.

So here is the secret of confidence... Confidence is not something you've got, or not got, it is something you do or don't do.

Confidence is just a 'state' and can be triggered, just like any other state at any time. Like any other skill, it's something you must practise.

Here is how to trigger your confidence whenever you want to:

- Think of a time when you were at your most confident ever. This might have been the best game you've ever played in, after winning something or some other significant time.

- Write down everything you can remember from this time. If possible write down what you were seeing, hearing and feeling in as much detail as possible.

- Close your eyes and revisit this confidence experience, making the feeling stronger and stronger until you can anchor it (*see* page 62).

- Now think of a time in the future when it would be useful to have this confidence. This might be a big game coming up or some other event when it is important to be at your best.

- Mentally practise this event going exactly as you would want it to (*see* page 75). Make sure that you get the feeling of confidence while doing the mental practice.

- Make this mental practice of confidence part of your routine. We recommend five minutes a day or twenty minutes twice a week, plus five minutes before each game.

'*Confidence is a habit that can be developed by acting as if you already had the confidence you desire to have.*' Brian Tracy, international speaker, consultant and author

KEY POINT TO REMEMBER

- Remember that the more you practise 'doing' confidence, the more of a habit it will become. Put simply, the more often you feel confident, the more confident you will feel.

CHAPTER 2
I CAN'T CONCENTRATE

Are you 'switched on' in training?

IMPROVING CONCENTRATION FOR GAMES

We'd recommend practising these techniques if you are the kind of player who 'switches off' during games, or if you often play well for 89 minutes, only to make a vital mistake when it really matters.

The first step in retraining your brain to focus for longer periods of time is probably the simplest, yet for many people can be the most difficult.

In a moment, close your eyes and focus only on your breathing. Count each breath, seeing how high you can count before you become distracted by other thoughts. By 'distracted', we don't mean 'losing count'. You must start again whenever a thought about anything other than the rise and fall of your breathing comes into your head.

It's not unusual for people to become distracted by the time they reach 10 the first time they do this exercise. You can consider yourself very good at it when you can count to 100 without your mind wandering.

To improve your focus, practise this at least twice a day until you get into three figures and ensure that you beat your previous 'record' each time.

Now think of around 10 things – very specific things – that you need to concentrate on during a game. The examples on pages 80–2 will help with this.

Do the breathing exercise above, but this time as you take a breath run one of the 10 scenarios through your mind. For example, breathe – heading the ball away – breathe – attacking a free kick in the box – breathe – making a cross-field run off the ball etc.

Mastering this allows you to keep focused on key tasks in the game while remaining completely relaxed.

IMPROVING CONCENTRATION FOR TRAINING

Some players are considered 'bad trainers'. Some of the most talented players we've ever worked with have gone through spells out of the team because they look like they are being lazy in training. In fact it's more often that the player hasn't been 'switched on' during the session.

If this sounds like you, then do the following.

Think of three to five small performance goals that you want to achieve during training. Performance goals are normally small technical targets such as ten accurate passes in a row, five consecutive shots on target or three 'nutmegs' during a small-sided game.

When you have decided on your targets, write the numbers related to them down on a wrist band or on the back of your hand. The writing should be small enough so others can't see but large enough so that you can. Ensure you remember what each number relates to.

Of course your main task is to make sure you do the drills that your coach sets out, but to keep your own interest and focus, look to achieve your own goals too.

GOAL SETTING, CONCENTRATION AND CONSISTENCY

The brain is wired to follow instructions that it is given. It will, even unconsciously, try to follow commands and find ways to achieve goals that have been set. (There is more on the relevance of this in Chapter 6 of this book.) It's because of this 'wiring' that setting goals and targets helps players to gain consistency and remain focused throughout the season.

To learn how to set goals in a way that is interesting, really engages the brain and therefore gets great results, see page 124.

'Concentration is the secret of strength.' Ralph Waldo Emerson, American essayist, poet, and leader of the Transcendentalist movement

KEY POINTS TO REMEMBER

- Developing your mental focus and concentration is like developing a muscle. The more you train yourself, the more focused you will become during games.
- Players who 'read the game well' are really just those who stay more focused on the game more of the time.

WHAT YOU FOCUS ON DIRECTLY AFFECTS YOUR PERFORMANCE

Craig Armstrong has had a successful career, having played in all four divisions at clubs including Nottingham Forest, Huddersfield Town, Sheffield Wednesday, Bradford City, Cheltenham Town and Gillingham. His views on the importance of mental fitness are clear.

'It is 99 per cent of what drives your game and your career,' he said. 'If you aren't mentally prepared, you just can't play well. Let's just say you are playing against someone who gave you a hard time the last time you played... if that is what you are focusing on, you will just get another hard time. You have got to focus on doing the right thing, playing well and, if need be, how you get others to support you during the game.

'Determination and focus are vital and they feed into each other. If you are focused you will be determined. Being determined leads to a great focus. I even find that talking others through the game helps to increase my focus, especially if I encourage them to be more determined.'

These mental skills are again mentioned by a seasoned professional, yet they are something that players are just expected to develop, rather than specifically being built up.

Craig continues: 'To make it as a professional player you must have some degree of talent, but look at the difference that extra desire can make. Robbie Savage has had a fantastic career; people will always say he hasn't got the ability of others, but in a way that is even more of a compliment. If he hasn't got ability then it is his massive desire to progress, be successful and win that has given him a successful career at club and international level.

'Then take someone like David Beckham. The time when money was a key driver for him passed long ago. It's not his bank balance that is pushing him to fly backwards and forwards from England to America for a game of football. It's the desire to continue performing for as long as possible. Even when he was still the first name on the England team sheet, he gave absolutely everything. Some players just don't have that drive.

If there is a way to develop this in young players, then we should. Because there are many moderately well off, exceptionally talented players out there who just can't seem to drive themselves on to the next level. That is really sad for everyone involved in the game.'

CHAPTER 3
I CAN'T GET MOTIVATED FOR THE GAME

What's your motivation?

This is a problem that players at all levels experience at some point in their career. Even the most passionate of players will at some point find it difficult to motivate themselves to perform at their usual level of intensity.

This dip in what is also known as 'activation' is usually experienced when you play against a team from a lower league or on a poor pitch. Occasionally though, this feeling of being 'flat' or lethargic can be as a result of being too activated for too long before the game so that by the time you've reached match day you are tired.

FIVE WAYS TO GET MORE MOTIVATED FOR A GAME

- Set yourself specific performance targets for the game (*see* page 21).
- Imagine that the person in your life that you would most like to see you play well is going to be there. Mentally rehearse the game as if you were playing in front of them until you feel more motivated to play well.
- Prepare for the game the way that you would if it was the biggest game of your life. This includes how you move around the dressing room, how you warm up and how you speak to your team mates. Even if you don't feel motivated at first, doing this will grow the feeling.
- Spend time before the game remembering three of the best performances of your life. See and hear the performances as if you were there again, until you get the feelings of excitement that you had during the game.
- Think about all the reasons you play football at all. If it's your job, think about the lifestyle it gives you and all the perks you get. If you play for pleasure, think about what playing gives you and how it makes you feel when you play well.

You might want to go back to the beginning of this book and re-read our example of these tools in action in the most intense of circumstances.

'The difference between the impossible and the possible lies in a person's determination.' Tommy Lasorda, former Major League baseball pitcher and manager

KEY POINTS TO REMEMBER

- There is a level of activation that is perfect for you when you play football. The more aware you can be of how you feel when you play at your very best, the easier it will be for you to motivate yourself to the correct level, without becoming too fired up.
- Another strategy is to think of what it would be like to never be allowed to play football again. This works for a smaller number of people, but can be useful as an additional tool.

CHAPTER 4
MY PERFORMANCES ARE INCONSISTENT

If you're suffering a dip in form, you need to re-programme your mind

CONSISTENT SUCCESS OVER A SEASON

How consistent are you? Every player has some peaks and dips in form, but do you go from outstanding to terrible even in the same game? Are you a striker that goes on goal-scoring runs, then droughts?

They say that form is temporary but class is permanent, but we have seen players have dips in form that last several seasons. Fans are often left wondering what happened to the 'superstar' player who now looks more like they belong in a Sunday league.

Before we give you the tools to minimise dips in form, let us say really clearly what *doesn't* happen. You definitely don't lose the physical skill and ability that you had. If you are physically fit enough to play the way you have in the past, the only thing that gets in the way is your mental state. Fix that and you'll get your form back.

WHY INCONSISTENCY HAPPENS

To put it in a nutshell, your brain gets in the way of your body doing what it is trained to do. When you are in the right mental state, your muscles will remember everything they are meant to do in a game situation. If you get too stressed or too relaxed, your mind will start releasing chemicals (such as corticotropin releasing factor – CRF) around the body that get in the way of this.

You can find lots more about activation, flow states and the many other scientific processes that cause this reaction in other books. But for now, here are two ways – programming future performance and the 'next ball' trigger – to maintain your form at a higher level for more of the time.

PROGRAMMING FUTURE PERFORMANCE

This process will help maintain your levels of performance over a number of games. The basic principle is similar to mental rehearsal but with a twist that programmes your mind, and therefore your body, even more effectively.

- Write the games you have over the next three months on separate pieces of paper.
- Place them on the floor in order with the next game closest to you and the last one furthest away. Each game should be one step apart.
- Stand at the beginning of the line of games and relax.
- Step on the first piece of paper and imagine you are playing in that game. See, hear and feel what it will be like to be playing outstandingly well in that fixture.
- When you are ready, step into the next game.
- Continue this until you have walked through each game.
- Once you've stepped off the final piece of paper, turn around and look back over each game. Imagine that you are now in the future and these games have gone exactly how you want them to have gone. Describe what you did that made this run of games so successful. It's important that you describe what happened in as much detail as possible and you talk about it as if it has already happened. If there is someone you can describe this to, then that is useful; if not, write it down. You should end up with something like Table 4.1 overleaf.

Why it works

As you will already know if you've read through other sections of this book, your brain will do everything it can to follow instructions. This walk-through enables your body to do what it needs to make these predictions come true. Creating the process as if it has already happened makes this much more powerful. In effect, you are confusing the brain (in a good way) so that when it comes to these games, you should do what you predicted more naturally.

TABLE 4.1 PROGRAMMING FUTURE PERFORMANCE

Match	What made it successful
Liverpool (H)	Started well, got a good tackle in early in the game. Distribution good throughout, won every header. Man of the match.
Wigan (A)	Stood up physically, talked throughout the game. Won most headers, blocked shot on the line.
Everton (H)	Scored, good passing throughout. Attacked ball well. Minimised threat from attacking midfielder.
Newcastle (A)	Relaxed before key game, started well. Defended long ball well. Talked well throughout. Singled out for praise on Match of the Day.
West Ham (H)	Kept the line high, good discipline when wound up. Defended set piece well. Good distribution, got forward when possible.

Walk back through each of the games reviewing your thoughts on each.

CONSISTENT SUCCESS DURING GAMES

Let's start with an obvious question. Is it easier to play a single pass or win a whole game? Naturally, playing a single pass, even a long one, is easier.

A really quick way for most players to maintain a high level of performance throughout games is to focus solely on the next pass, tackle, header or shot that you need to make.

Any player will perform best when they are in a 'flow state' (more often known as being 'in the zone'). When you are in 'flow', time will pass without you realising and even the most difficult skills will be effortless.

'Flow' happens when there is a balance between how much skill you have and how difficult the game is. If you are an outstanding player, playing in a tough game, you will be at your best.

If you're finding the game difficult, or if you have other things playing on your mind, you'll feel stressed and therefore won't be able to perform at the top of your game.

If the game is too easy for you, or if you are overconfident, your mind becomes bored and you lose focus or try to do more difficult things.

THE 'NEXT BALL' TRIGGER

In various sections of this book, we've looked at various techniques for mentally rehearsing specific skills and phases of play. Whether you've done that or not, focusing on the next ball will help you get into the 'zone' more often.

This is a simple reminder during any game to focus only on the very next specific thing that you have to do during the game. When you focus only on the next ball your conscious mind pays attention to this and your unconscious mind allows your muscle memory to do what it is trained to.

Whenever you notice your mind wandering during the game or your performance dipping, start saying 'next ball' to yourself. Keep your focus only on the next pass, header, shot or tackle until you have played your way back into the game.

This simple tool becomes extremely powerful when combined with other tools in the book such as positive mental rehearsal, positive language and creating future histories.

'Without consistency there is no moral strength.'
Robert Owen, Welsh social reformer

KEY POINTS TO REMEMBER

- To be truly effective, any goal-setting must be multi-sensory. Logically thought-out targets written on paper only tap into a small part of the mind's capacity to make sure we achieve them.
- 'Wow' goals are those that make you smile when you think about what it would be like to have achieved them. Try setting some of these: you will be amazed how close you get to them.
- Reviewing your aims to see what you have achieved is a great way to be motivated to do even more.

CHAPTER 5
SOMETIMES I JUST LOSE IT

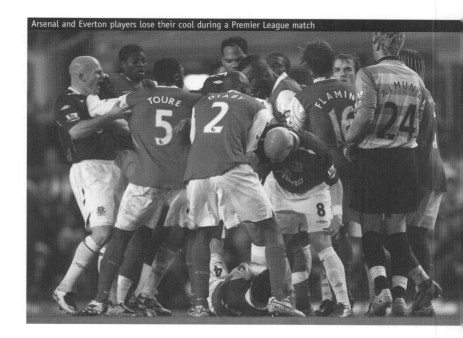

Arsenal and Everton players lose their cool during a Premier League match

Football at any level is a high-intensity, physical sport. There will be times when keeping calm is difficult and your temper can take over. This chapter is especially for those players who can just 'lose it' following a foul, a referee's decision or even something a team mate has done.

As with most of the tools and techniques in this book, it will take some practice. But if you are willing to focus on it, this process will help you to keep cool even in the most challenging of situations.

WHY THIS TECHNIQUE WORKS

Feelings move around your body. They must do, otherwise we would not be able to feel them. Changing the direction of the feeling will change the nature of the feeling. This is all to do with electro-chemical reactions in the body causing emotional responses (to understand more about this, see page 55). These next five steps focus on identifying where a feeling starts and which direction it moves in, before changing the direction to put you back in control.

FOUR STEPS TO STAYING IN CONTROL

- Think of a specific time when you were playing or training and you really 'lost it'.
- Run the situation through in your head as if you were there again. See what you saw and hear what you heard until you begin to get the feeling again that you had when it actually happened.
- Focus on the feeling that you are getting.
  - ○ Where in your body does the feeling start? (You might have to run the memory through in your head until you are sure you have got the starting point.)
  - ○ Now notice which direction the feeling is moving in. Is it upwards, clockwise, downwards or from side to side? What tension does this movement create?
  - ○ As soon as you notice tension beginning, practise making the feeling go in a different direction. For example, if you notice the feeling starting in your chest and moving up to create a tension in your head, make the feeling

move down from your head to your stomach instead. You'll feel the difference straight away.

- Repeat this until you feel calm when you think of the original situation.

- Repeat this with another example in your head until whenever you think of a time that you were annoyed, you can catch the feeling and get in control quickly.

SOME EXAMPLES

'Anger for me is a huge tension that runs down my shoulder into my hands. My fists clench and, if I let it build, something will get hit. But the feeling starts in my jaw. My first reaction is that my teeth clench and my jaw tightens. If, as soon as it starts, I open my mouth, relaxing my jaw, it's almost impossible to keep the feeling of "angry" going.' Richard

Chasing the Referee

We worked with a very highly rated young player in his first year as a senior professional who was already getting a reputation for chasing referees and pushing arguments too far.

Using the first part of the process, we identified that the feeling (he called it 'injustice') started in his arms and chest and moved upwards to his head. This explained why he threw his arms up in the air when he argued. We coached him so that whenever the feeling started, he would breathe out hard.

Breathing out hard, of course, pushes his chest and shoulders down and helps keep his arms by his side. Simply by doing this, even when thinking about big 'injustices' caused by referees, he stopped the feelings. This in turn stopped the bookings and fines and even the arguments with his team mates.

'The worst-tempered people I've ever met were the people who knew they were wrong.' Wilson Mizner, American playwright and entrepreneur

KEY POINTS TO REMEMBER

- Is it possible to lose your temper and keep completely focused on playing at the top of your game? If you really chase the referee, is he more likely to give you decisions?
- We all know that the answer to these questions is 'no', and that a loss of control is never helpful. So learning this technique is not just about staying calm. It is about keeping yourself in the right frame of mind to perform at your best.
- Mastering this technique will also reduce the amount of fines you pay and the number of games you miss through suspension.

MENTAL FITNESS IN SOCCER – A VIEW FROM TOP SOCCER COACHES IN THE UNITED STATES

Mental Toughness Is Key

The San Diego Surf Soccer Club is widely recognised as one of the premier youth soccer clubs in the United States. Over the years, Surf teams have won 46 State Cup championships. In fact, Surf is consistently ranked among the top five clubs in the nation by GOT Soccer (the US soccer statistics organisation), based on the impressive results of Surf's boys and girls teams from Under-11 through to Under-19. In 2003, Surf teams captured a national championship, three regional championships, numerous state championships and top-tier tournament titles. Colin Chesters is Surf's Director of Coaching and a former professional with Derby County and Crewe Alexandra.

He shares his thoughts on the importance of mental toughness to a successful playing career.

'Being mentally tough is so important because the game is full of ups and downs, highs and lows,' says Colin. 'Being able to rebound from a tough loss where you might have missed an easy chance or penalty is crucial. Having the right mental skills to cope with these situations could help thousands of players to go further in the game.

'The best modern-day examples of players demonstrating this resilience are David Beckham and Cristiano Ronaldo. After Beckham's disastrous 2006 World Cup and the start of his Real Madrid 2006-07 season he recovered and is probably the most admired player in world football. What about the thoughts going on in Cristiano Ronaldo's head after being somewhat responsible for England's demise in the 2006 World Cup? The thought of playing in England the following season and being booed at every stadium, and worse, would have seen a mentally weak player head off to pastures new. These players went on to rebound in the most positive ways with fantastic seasons.

'Players not as mentally strong might be picking up a pay cheque with a club in the lower leagues right now.

'The most important mental skill is letting go of mistakes right after they happen and not letting them build up. If this happens, players don't feel like they want to touch the ball again for fear of making yet another mistake. We must help players to let it go and focus on the next task. You can't go back and fix the last mistake, but you can learn from it.

'I truly believe that, if I had known there were ways to alter your state of mind and better ways to dismiss mistakes when I was given my chance at Derby in the late 1970s, I might have been a household name. So it's really important to me to pass this knowledge on to the talented players I work with here.'

Another decorated US soccer coach echoes Colin's views. Steve Cook is the Program Director for North County United Soccer Club and is a four-time State Cup winner with his previous club, Del Mar Sharks. Having come through the ranks at Newcastle United, he also played in the US for Kansas City Wizards and has recently been training with LA Galaxy in a bid to overcome a knee injury that interrupted his playing career.

Steve believes that players must begin developing these key mental skills at a young age. He comments: 'Young players don't necessarily know the game as naturally as in Europe, so it's especially important to have them think about what they are doing during practices and why they are doing it. What is interesting is the speed at which the players begin to coach each other on particular skills.'

While in the States, we watched Steve coach a group of Under-11 girls. Their decision-making was exceptional for their age, as was their use of the ball. What impressed us most was, as Steve points out, the fact that the girls almost coach each other. The whole session had a very different feel to similar sessions we've watched in the UK.

Steve continues: 'We understand over here that it's not just about physical, technical and tactical development. If we want players to develop into competitive soccer players, we must prepare them for the mental stress this causes. And while we bring in specialists to help the players, it is even more important to us that the coaches and parents have the skills and knowledge to continue this development on a regular basis.'

Liverpool's Djibril Cissé places the ball on the spot during the penalty
shootout in the 2005 Champions League final against AC Milan

PART 2: USEFUL TOOLS AND TECHNIQUES

CHAPTER 6
USING LANGUAGE EFFECTIVELY

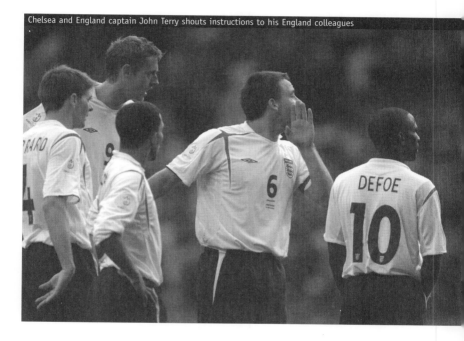

Chelsea and England captain John Terry shouts instructions to his England colleagues

'See, I told you that you were rubbish. You look forward to the game all week, it's finally here and you screw up your big chance.' Are these comments familiar? You would expect them to come from an old-school manager or an over-critical parent, but the truth of it is that you said them… to yourself.

Our voice is the one we hear most often and that is why it rules our life. It influences everything from our achievements to our physical fitness, and from our relationships to the decisions we make.

'DON'T PICTURE WAYNE ROONEY NAKED'

You did, didn't you? But we said 'don't'! You've just discovered the first key factor about language. The brain is designed to follow commands. It searches for them, even when we try to hide them. In order for you not to picture Wayne Rooney in the nude, you must first imagine the image and then try to wipe it away. This is the way we are built.

The second key aspect is that the body and brain are all one 'system'. Candice Pert, who was nominated for the Nobel Prize for Women in Science, said 'the brain is located within and throughout the body'.

This means that when you receive information it doesn't just go into the brain, it goes into the body. What then happens if you tell yourself 'you're crap', 'that's terrible', 'you are having a nightmare'? Your body takes that information as a command and will try to honour it. There is an old computer term: garbage in, garbage out. The same can be said of the brain (and body).

The messages that we send around the nervous system are so vital that they influence not just our performance on the pitch but our lives off it. For example, what happens when we consistently say 'I'm tired'? Your brain sends this message around the body and it responds by creating more 'tired' feelings. This in turn returns a message to the brain that the body is tired, and this is recognised by the brain as tiredness, which is recognised by you. The next time someone asks you how you are, you may respond 'really tired', and the process continues, getting worse each time.

Imagine the impact then of changing your internal and external language in this situation to 'I could really do with more energy'. Think about how the process would work in these circumstances and what the results would be.

This concept shows why language, both internal and external, what we say to others and ourselves, is so crucial to our success in football. Imagine the impact of telling yourself 'I just can't score'.

Most people would expect professional players to avoid this kind of unhelpful internal chatter. Our experience is that even the best fall into the trap at some time in their career.

What would happen then if you trained yourself so that your language was filled with positive commands to your body and brain? Three things happened when I changed my language:

- I had more confidence and energy when playing.
- I became more consistent.
- My teams won more games when I played, even though the other players who played in my position had more ability. (I believe this is due to the more useful focus the rest of the team had because of the language I used on the pitch.)

Consider the impact on your performance if, when you realise that things could be going better, you told yourself 'keep working hard and enjoying the game and you'll be great,' that 'the next pass will be a good one', 'the next shot will be on target', or 'you will win the next tackle'. This is not about positive fluffy chat. It is about helping your body to do what it has been trained to do.

EXTERNAL LANGUAGE

Of course, all of this also applies to the language you use with other people. Their brains search for commands too. They'll discard the 'don't's, 'avoid's and 'stop's. So when you shout 'don't give the ball away', their brains delete 'don't' and respond with 'okay, I'll try to give the ball away.' When you tell them at half-time 'we've got to stop giving them the ball', or when you scream 'don't dive in', their brains will focus on doing exactly the thing you are trying to avoid.

What are we doing to players around us if we tell them they are 'crap', 'a waste of space' or precede criticism with 'You always…' (for example, screw up or go to sleep on set pieces)? Yet again, we are just programming these things in. Unless their internal dialogue is really powerful, it will have a negative impact on their performance.

TRY THIS...

Have a go at coming up with some alternative suggestions to the phrases opposite. Remember the aim is to get the same message across but using a more useful command.

Our suggestions are at the end of the chapter.

WHAT IS HELPFUL LANGUAGE, AND WHAT IS NOT

One of the questions we regularly get asked by managers about language is: 'That's all very well and good, but what about when they really have been terrible?'

TABLE 6.1 HELPFUL LANGUAGE

Unhelpful Language	What you could say instead...
We always play badly on this ground	
Don't give the ball away	
Don't concede	
Stop diving in	
Don't lose your cool	
That is terrible	
I keep missing the target	
This pitch is no good for us	
It's a pressure game	
Whatever you do don't (freeze, chuck it etc)	
Add some of your own...	

Let us be clear. Positive or useful language is not about being 'nice' all the time. Nor is it avoiding being critical. If swearing is normal where you play, we're not judging that (it's okay: you can still swear if you feel it's necessary). Saying it right is about giving information in a way that increases the likelihood of players improving and doing what is required. If you are a player the same applies. It's about giving yourself the right message to help you perform at your best.

Helpful language gives attention to what is required and how to improve. Unhelpful language concentrates on what's bad and has already gone wrong.

You can, when you think it's appropriate, still give your players (or yourself) a roasting while using positive language.

Compare these two team talks:

Right we were terrible last week and I won't stand for it if you do that again today. You never got going and that gave them the initiative. Don't stand off them again, don't waste possession and don't mess about with it at the back.

No more high balls into nowhere. You just lost your heads last week. I don't want to see that again or you'll be off. This is a huge game so don't make mistakes.

Okay, we weren't at our best last week, but we can make amends this week. You can start much stronger and you've got to take the game to them. Get stuck in, win your tackles, keep the ball and use it properly. If you need to clear the ball at the back, do it. You must keep the ball on the ground and it is important that you hit it to feet. Keep your heads and stay relaxed. This is your chance to make amends:

make the most of it. It is a big game and if you stay focused on doing the right things we will win.

Which is more likely to be helpful? Which is more likely to produce a positive result? Which is most like you?

KEY POINTS TO REMEMBER

- Our own voice rules us – use it to talk to your brain and body in the most appropriate way.
- We are programmed to follow commands – make them the right ones
- Turn negative commands into positive ones.
- Think and talk about what can be done to make improvements.
- Ask for what you want, not what you don't.

TABLE 6.2 CHANGE YOUR LANGUAGE

Unhelpful Language	What you could say instead...
We always play badly on this ground	Let's break the pattern here today, OR This is just like every other ground we've ever won on
Don't give the ball away	Keep the ball

Unhelpful Language	What you could say instead...
Don't concede	Keep it tight, OR Defend well, OR Keep a clean sheet
Stop diving in	Stand up, OR Stay on your feet
Don't lose your cool	Keep your temper, OR Stay calm
That is terrible	We've got to do a hell of a lot better
I keep missing the target	The next one will be in, OR I'm going to get a goal today
This pitch is no good for us	Let's make the most of the conditions, OR Let's make sure we do the right things on this pitch
It's a pressure game	This is a great opportunity, OR It's really important we stay focused
Whatever you do don't (freeze, chuck it etc)	Make the most of this opportunity, OR Do your best, OR Focus on doing your job well

Remember this is not so much about what is positive or not, it is about what is negative or not.

Begin to change your language immediately. The longer you wait, the more time it will take to change. Start immediately and soon you and the people around you will have the extra advantage just through the words that you use.

CHAPTER 7
TRIGGERING STATES AND USING ANCHORS

Scotland line up for photos in the moments before kick-off in a European Championship qualifier aganst Italy

Let's start this chapter with a quick overview of what we mean by states.

States are the physical and emotional feelings you have throughout the body as a result of changes in your focus (what you're thinking about), physiology (anything to do with the body and movement) and the language that you use.

This basic idea should become imprinted on your brain now because it's the basis of so much that affects your performance and therefore your career. You don't need us to tell you that the mood (or state) you are in makes a difference to your conversations on and off the pitch. It impacts on how you train and play. In fact, people who study the impact of states would say that states run our lives.

So if that is true, imagine how useful it would be to be able instantly to change the state you are in. Can you see the benefit of knowing what your ideal state is for before, during and after games, and to be able to trigger that state at any moment?

This chapter will show you exactly how to do that. It is split into two sections. Section one, 'Knowing your states and using existing anchors', is really for those of you new to these ideas. Section two, 'Creating new anchors', describes how to devise even more anchors to help you and your team mates.

KNOWING YOUR STATES AND USING EXISTING ANCHORS

How do you feel right now?

Most of you will answer 'Fine', 'Okay' or 'Not too bad' (unless you've just read the chapter on language, of course!) We want you to think more carefully: how do you *actually* feel? What feelings do you have in your body as you think about it now? Where do you feel them? What direction are the feelings moving in?

Now you've paid more attention to the feelings you've really got, give them a name. That's the *state* you are really in.

It may seem like an unusual thing to ask you to do, but the first step for most people in being able to trigger states more effectively is to be able to identify which state they are in to start with.

The next thing to understand is that there are no 'right' or 'wrong' states. Most states can be useful depending on the situation. It is fairly obvious to say that different states are more or less useful at different times.

For example, high-energy states are really useful most of the time during a game, but not the night before when you're trying to rest up. Similarly, low-energy states are very useful when recovering from training or between games, but much less helpful during a high-intensity fitness session.

So to recap:

- States are the feelings you have in your body.
- They are triggered by changes in what you think about, how you move or what you say.
- Most states can be useful; the secret is to know which state is best for the situation.

Knowing Your Best States

Use the table overleaf to help you identify the states you'd like to be able to trigger at key times. We've included a state menu on page 72 to give you some inspiration.

If you have done the exercise in the table, we're certain that you'll have a mix of high-energy and low-energy states. There'll also be some instances where you might not be able to describe the state in words, but you know exactly what it feels like. All of this is okay: we're all different and it doesn't really matter what you call the state as long as you know what it is and you can trigger it when you want.

TABLE 7.1 THE RIGHT STATE AT THE RIGHT TIME

Key activity or situation	Your ideal state
The night before a game	
Travelling to the game	
During the warm-up	
Five minutes to kickoff	
As the game kicks off	
Taking a penalty	
The referee gives a penalty against you and you know your opponent dived	
Your team mate misses an open goal then blames you for a bad pass	
At half-time, the manager is going through the first half and being really critical	
Straight after the game you're asked to do a live interview on TV or radio	
In the evening after a heavy defeat you have to attend a family function	

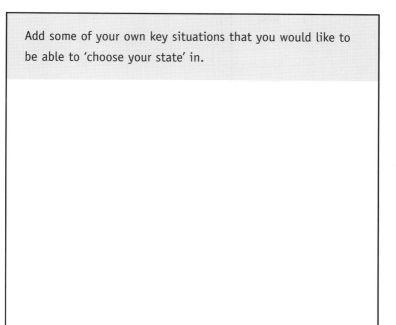

Add some of your own key situations that you would like to be able to 'choose your state' in.

Your Anchors

Put simply, anchors are triggers that set off changes in state. We all have anchors already.

For example, think of your favourite food, something that you just love the smell and taste of. Think about the last time that food was cooked to perfection for you. Imagine it being set down in front of you, perfectly ready to be eaten. The chances are you are salivating right now even though the food isn't actually in front of you. That's because your favourite food is an anchor. It creates a change in state and for most people this will be both physiological (salivating) and in focus (thinking about when you are going to eat next).

Think about your favourite piece of music. When you think about times in the past when you've listened to this music, what memories are triggered? If you played that music now, how would you feel? You may even be starting to experience a little of that feeling already.

So you can see you've already got some anchors that you can access pretty easily. In fact, you have hundreds of these: all you need to do now is remember what they are and use them at the right times.

In other chapters we talk more about the importance of the different senses when it comes to mental fitness. The most useful way we've found to identify existing anchors is by sense. Use the table on page 61 to identify your existing anchors and the states they generate.

Matching Your Anchors To Your Ideal States

Many people find that by doing the previous two exercises they discover that they already have an existing anchor for the majority of 'ideal' states. If this isn't the case, then you'll discover how to generate more anchors in the second part of this chapter.

It is important to remember that the brain doesn't differentiate well between what is real and what is strongly imagined. This means, for example, that if a picture of a member of your family gives you the feeling of motivation that you need just before you start training, then you have a choice. You can either carry the picture around with you and look at it just before you train, or you can picture it really clearly in your head. Both will trigger the feeling that you want.

TABLE 7.2 KNOWING YOUR ANCHORS

Think of as many things as you can that change how you feel when you see, hear, touch, smell or taste them. These could be pictures, places, people, music, food or objects. Think of some that generate high-energy states and some that generate low-energy states. Next to each one, write the state that anchor generates.

Existing anchor	State it generates
Example: The track 'Trouble With Me' reminds me of my favourite 'lads' holiday.	Very relaxed and chilled out.

CREATING NEW ANCHORS

In this section we'll look at how you can set up more anchors to enable you to be in the best state for any key activity at any time.

It is important that you know the basics of states and anchoring before you begin using this simple process. If this is the first time you've come across the term 'anchoring', we'd suggest you read part one of this chapter first.

Simple Anchoring

The simplest way to create an anchor is 'in the moment'. For example, the next time you have an outstanding game, feel exceptionally relaxed or experience any other feeling you'd like to be able to access at any time, make a specific movement such as squeezing your forefinger and thumb together or playing a specific piece of music.

Remember that mastering this technique will put you in charge of your feelings. With a little time, effort and practice you will be able to feel however you want, whenever you want to. Imagine the impact that would have on your performances and your career.

When creating anchors, it's important to capture the state at its peak, so set your anchor when the feeling is at its most intense.

FIGURE 7.1 ANCHORING PEAK PERFORMANCE

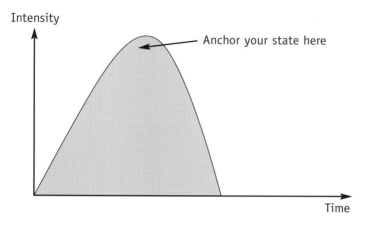

Re-accessing and Anchoring

It's great if you can anchor in the moment; the challenge though, is remembering to do it.

You can relax though because anchors can also be created after the event has taken place using the following process. By doing this, you can create as many anchors to as many states as you possibly want.

So here is how you can create an anchor to generate any state you want, whenever you want to. You can either go through this process yourself or, if you've got someone who can coach you through it, that can be even more powerful.

1   *Identify* the state you want to anchor (for example, confidence).

2   *Access* the state by thinking back to a time when you felt totally confident. Really go back and relive the experience intensely. If you feel you have never in your life experienced

total confidence, it's still okay. Just imagine it. Alternatively, step into the shoes of the most confident person you know. It can even be somebody you've never met. The important thing is to make the experience as intense as you can. After a few seconds, stop and think about something totally different for a few seconds. Re-access the state a few times until you are sure you can intensify it and know how to create a peak state.

3   Just as the state is peaking... *introduce your anchor*. This can be a picture, a word or phrase said in a particular tone, a piece of music, or a particular touch or gesture. Repeat this a few times, making sure that you keep or increase the intensity of the feeling. Make sure this trigger is precise, easy to reproduce and that it is unique and not something you use everyday.

4   Think about something else for a few seconds, then focus on your new anchor by triggering it and noticing the feeling you get.

For some people going through this process may seem a bit of a chore, so now seems like a good time to remind you of a few key points:

● Your state affects every other part of your game, from your form to how you recover from injury, from how you train to how you feel about your manager or coach.

● This process allows you to feel how you want to, when you want to, without any other external help.

● Most people acknowledge that the mental side of football is at least as important as the technical, tactical and physical aspects. If this is the case, it is worth spending ten minutes a day developing your mental technique.

'Physical strength is a bonus ... mental strength is a must.'
Viraf Avari, chess player and coach

KEY POINTS TO REMEMBER

- States run our lives. How we feel governs what we do at all times, not just on the pitch.
- States are like the weather: they change constantly. We just don't realise it most of the time. Putting yourself in charge of how you feel is one of the most powerful things you can ever do – imagine what it would be like knowing that nobody could ever make you feel bad ever again because you choose your state, regardless of what they say or do.
- This can be achieved by focusing on the three pillars that have been mentioned throughout this book: focus, physiology and language.
- Begin to become aware of your states right now and make this a key element of your daily routine. It will change your life.

CHAPTER 8
RELAXATION AND DEALING WITH NERVES

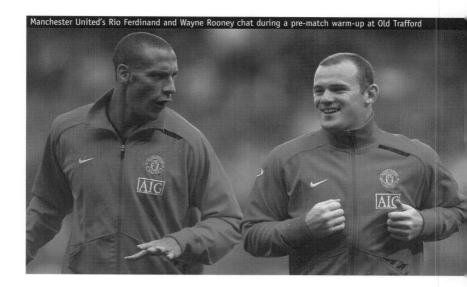

Manchester United's Rio Ferdinand and Wayne Rooney chat during a pre-match warm-up at Old Trafford

RELAXATION

How do you relax? For most people it's about getting a beer and watching the TV, but actually this isn't enough to give your body a proper rest.

Even though footballers are generally much fitter than the average person, it's hugely important to dedicate some very specific time to allowing your heart rate to return to normal and your body to recover after exercise.

Most of the professionals we work with actually have pretty bad sleeping patterns. They aren't able to relax totally before games so they don't sleep well. Often they don't return until late after games and again spend time thinking about the match, meaning they don't get to sleep until four or five the following morning.

Remember that it's during times of sleep or deep relaxation that muscles repair themselves most and that the brain processes the memories of the day and 'clears itself', ready for tomorrow.

Having a clear relaxation pattern is vital if your sleep pattern isn't consistent. Something that we teach to almost all our clients is a breathing technique that helps to reset your body to a natural relaxed state. In fact, research has shown that breathing techniques can help reduce pain and blood pressure, increase fitness, and are good for the heart, digestive system and brain. It can help you to sleep, to reduce stress, to focus before a game and is especially good if you're going to do some mental rehearsal (*see* page 75). It's very simple to do but comes highly recommended by every player we know who uses it.

So here's the technique:

1   Breathe in for your own count of eight.
2   Hold the breath in for your own count of eight.
3   Breathe out for your own count of eight. Make sure you breathe all of the air out; you might need to 'push' it out.
4   Hold, with no air in, for your own count of four.
5   Repeat steps 1 – 4 twice more.

That is the technique. It's very simple and very powerful. Try it and see how relaxed you feel.

USING MUSIC TO RELAX

The effect of music on the brain has been studied and understood for many years. There is a huge amount of research available that gives a much more detailed and scientific insight into the impact of music.

The purpose of this section is to give you a short, easy-to-use guide to how music can help or hinder your relaxation.

Your brain waves and heart rate will try to align themselves to the beats-per-minute of a piece of music. This is why music is used to motivate players before a game. You can use the same principle to relax. Music that is slower and has fewer beats-per-minute will reduce your heart rate and relax your mind.

You don't have to like the music for it to help you relax. For example, the ideal music to create a 'daydreamy' type of state is slow baroque music (a type of classical music). Our guess is that it's not what you've currently got on your MP3 player, but if it works then maybe you should give it a try. However, there is no point in choosing music that really irritates you – by nature, you won't relax. Try different types of 'New Age' music or some of the 'Chill Out' compilations until you find something that really works for you.

Use music in a planned way. Think about when you need to relax more and when you need to raise your state. Music is a fantastic tool for helping you to do this. So have a list of tracks available, some of them that raise your state, some of them that chill you out and some that completely relax you. Use them as and when you need.

DEALING WITH NERVES

Let's start with a quick explanation of what causes 'nerves'.

When we imagine things being difficult or going wrong, the brain kicks into 'fight or flight' and releases the adrenaline and other chemicals around the body that prepare it for what might happen next.

The crucial part of this is 'imagine things being difficult or going wrong'. In effect, it is impossible to feel nervous or fearful unless we imagine the potential bad things that could happen.

So if you want to cure your nerves, simply imagine everything going perfectly.

Is it that easy? Well it can be with some practice, if you train yourself to mentally rehearse fantastically well (*see* page 75.) To take this idea to the extreme, if someone walked into the room now and held a knife to you, it would be natural to be nervous or scared. The fear is not of the knife; it is of what might happen next. Nerves in football only appear when you imagine things going badly.

There is another complication in the process. There is very little difference between the feeling of fear and the feeling of excitement. If you are very excited you get out of breath, your heart races, your palms sweat, you perhaps have 'butterflies' in your stomach and your mind wanders. Now compare this to what happens when you get very nervous: the responses are the same. So you could say that dealing with fear is just about labelling it as excitement.

ADOPTING THE PHYSIOLOGY OF CONFIDENCE

Chapter 7 includes specific strategies to trigger your confidence. But, in addition to those, one way to deal with nerves if they creep up on you is to practise adopting the physiology of confidence – in other words, standing the way you stand if you are at your most confident ever.

Think about this. Who is the most confident player that you know? How do you know that they are confident? How would somebody who has just met them know? People who are seen as confident will demonstrate similar characteristics, most of which can easily be replicated by anyone.

Typical Physiological Characteristics of Confidence

- Straight posture
- Positive movements (whether attacking or defending)
- Even breath
- Firm, positive gestures
- Steadiness of vocal tone (rather than 'defensive tones' or 'screeching')

Being able to copy these characteristics allows more than a simple 'mimicking' of confidence. When anyone regularly adopts the physiology of confidence, they are encouraging their body to trigger confidence chemicals and electrical activity to stimulate a genuine state of confidence rather than fear or nervousness. It is very difficult to feel nervous while being in this physiology.

A MENU OF STATES

Here is a menu of states that you might want to get yourself into now that you have all the tools to do that.

MORE USEFUL STATES

Amused Amorous Aroused Abundant Amazed Awesome Adventurous Alright Autonomous Bemused Brilliant Bountiful Blooming Beguiled Clever Celebratory Careful Cosy Comfortable Carefree Calm Charged Cheerful Chilled Confident Congruent Creative Crafty Curious Delicious Delightful Deep Delectable Dreamy Ecstatic Elated Elegant Easy Empowered Energetic Energised Enigmatic Enthusiastic Excellent Excited Free Fine Fantastic Frivolous Funny Feminine Funky Grand Great Gregarious Glad Gigantic Good Giddy Giggly Gobsmacked Glutted Happy Healthy Heady High Hopeful Immense Important Intense Infallible Joyous Jubilant Kind-hearted Kissable Kooky Knowledgeable Kingly Loving Light-hearted Limber Loose Luminous Magnificent Magnanimous Magical Masterful Marvellous Masculine Nice Needed Natural Normal Nurtured Nurturing Open Passionate Playful Peace of mind Pleasure Powerful Proud Primed Peaceful Prayerful Protected Quiet Quixotic Queenly Quenched Ready Relaxed Right Restless Rested Scintillated Silly Sexy Surprised Switched-on Tasty Tempted Together Triumphant Tittilated Ten-times-better Trusting Understood Unbelievable Unstoppable Velvety Vibrant VaVaVoom! Vivacious Well Wonderful Wacky Way out Weird Wild Wicked Xtragoodtoday Young Youthful Zen-like

LESS USEFUL STATES

Annoyed Angry Animosity Abandoned Bad Bored Baffled Blue
Barren Base Blah Betrayed Cantankerous Crusty Crabby Cranky
Crappy Curmudgeonly Down Dark Dead(!) Degraded Dejected
Defenceless Defensive Defeated Disgruntled Desperate
Disgusted Embarrassed Frustrated Guarded Glutted Impotent
Knackered Lethargic Limited Lazy Malevolent Manic Mad
Miserable Morbid Misunderstood Nasty Obliged Obnoxious
Overworked Overtired Overwhelmed Off colour Offended Old
Pants Pathetic Pitiful Powerless Possessive Ragged Rickety
Resentful Raw Sad Sick Sorrowful Sapped Strange Stupid
Stupefied Stumped Screwy Terrible Tricked Timid Unsavoury
Under the weather Wimpy Wasted Wound up Xenophobic
Zzzzzzzz...

KEY POINTS TO REMEMBER

- In other areas of this book, we have mentioned
  'activation'. This is the state of readiness for performance,
  and there is an optimum level of activation for you to
  perform at your best.
- However, the body has a natural rise and fall of energy
  levels and it is unnatural for it to be kept at a high level
  of activation for a long period of time.
- In order to make the most of your activation peaks, you
  must be able to relax completely.

CHAPTER 9

POSITIVE MENTAL PRACTICE

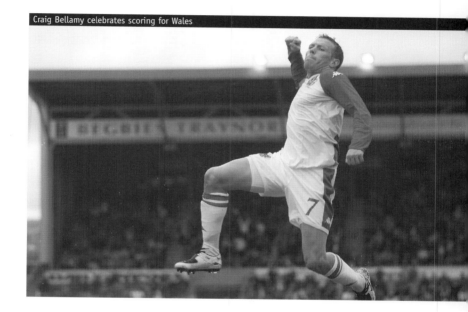

Craig Bellamy celebrates scoring for Wales

SEEING, HEARING AND FEELING YOURSELF DOING WELL

How many hours, days, weeks and months do you spend on the training ground making sure you're physically ready for the big games? How long do you spend in the gym with your conditioning coach and nutritionist?

How much time have you spent in the last month with your 'mental coach' making sure that your head is ready for the next big game? How much time have you spent mentally rehearsing?

While the body is finely tuned and well looked after, the mind – which, let's face it, drives your body – is often neglected.

There is so much research about the importance and bene-fit of mental practice, but this book isn't intended to be a scientific manifesto, written to give you proof. There are a tonne of those, lying untouched on the shelves.

Let's give you some headline hows and whys on the power of mental practice.

- The brain does not differentiate between what is real and what is strongly imagined. When you mentally rehearse, the brain creates the same reactions in your body as if the event has really happened. If you need proof of this, remember the last time you had a really bad dream? You will have woken up breathing heavily and sweating as if it were real.
- Your muscles have 'memory'. If someone pretended to throw you a ball now, you'd try to catch it without 'think-ing'. That's (partly) to do with muscle memory.
- If you mentally rehearse a skill – let's say finishing under pressure – you are programming your brain and your body to do this for real.
- Four out of five of our professional clients say that mental practice, along with relaxation, has made the biggest differ-ence in their performance.
- You can mentally rehearse any conditions. It's a pet hate of ours when we hear managers and players saying, 'You can't practise penalties'. You can. You can recreate the feeling and the pressure in your head at any time. If you practise mental rehearsal enough, you can quickly re-create and manage any feeling in any situation.

- As well as increasing skill, mental practice will increase focus, control, confidence, motivation and allow you to relax more.

MENTAL PRACTICE OR VISUALISATION?

What's the most vivid memory from your career so far? Think about that now. For most of you it will be your greatest success or your proudest moment.

As you think about it, focus on your memory. What are you seeing? What are the pictures like? Can you hear anything? What feelings are you getting?

Everyone is different, so the pictures, sounds and feelings you get will be different too. What we are sure of is that you won't just have had a single black-and-white 'photo', that flashed through your head and represented your most vivid memory. By nature, a vivid memory will be represented in a number of senses – some of you will have even been able to taste and smell the memory.

This process shows why you must mentally rehearse rather than just visualise. Good mental rehearsal is the future in HD surround sound; visualisation is the future with the sound turned off.

Visualisation uses just one of the senses. Mental rehearsal uses all of them and increases the chances of you getting what you want by programming the brain more effectively.

WHICH SENSE ARE YOU IN?

Think of your favourite ever holiday. What are the first three things that come to mind? Is it pictures of the beach or the pool? Perhaps it's the snow on the mountains? Maybe it's the look on the faces of the people around you at a certain point in the holiday?

For others it will be the feelings you had. The heat of the sun or the coolness of the water as you dive into the pool. It might just be a sense of relaxation, happiness or contentment.

Or did your memory go back to a favourite song first? Perhaps it's the sound of laughter and singing during a night out?

While we think and remember in all of the senses, at different times most people have a preference for one sense over the others. So if you are a 'visual', you'll be able to picture things more clearly. Hearing people will remember the sounds first, and feeling people (also called kinaesthetic people) will remember feelings.

MENTAL PRACTICE — A SECRET

Most people believe that mental practice is something you've got to learn. Here's the secret. You already do it. You will, we guarantee, spend some time before a game running what is going to happen through your head. You'll see, hear and/or feel some of the things that are going to happen at key points. We all do it.

So learning to do it isn't what you need; learning to do it *positively* is.

Think about the next really big game you have. If you allow yourself time to run through what might happen in the game, do you imagine all the good things that might happen – a great tackle, winning headers, scoring the winning goal? Or do you imagine things going wrong – the missed tackle, being beaten in the air or missing the penalty?

You see, that's the power of this technique. It can help you get what you really do want or it can help you get what you really don't want.

To begin with... If you're new to mental practice, we'd suggest you set just five minutes aside every day for two weeks or so to practise it until it becomes a habit and something that you can do any time and anywhere.

So go somewhere quiet where you can relax without being interrupted.

- Close your eyes.
- Relax – use a breathing technique from Chapter 8.
- Think about a specific situation that is coming up; let's use a game as an example.
- Run it through your head as if it was happening now. Make sure you are seeing things through your own eyes, rather than as if you where watching yourself on a screen.
- Start as early as is useful to you; we'd recommend starting at your arrival at the ground. See yourself arriving relaxed and on time, then move on to your preparation for the game, the warm-up and final team talk.
- Remember everything you see, hear and feel must be positive. If anything unhelpful sneaks in, rewind and see it again in a helpful way.
- Think about going out on to the pitch, the reaction from the crowd (only the helpful stuff), then the game itself.

- Most people don't rehearse every kick of every minute of the game; instead focus on key aspects of the game and create possible situations in your mind that you want to be prepared for.

Here are examples of specific areas of the game that some of our clients rehearse. We've organised them based on their position on the pitch.

Examples of mental practice by position

Goalkeeper
- First catch – clean and it sticks
- First clearance from the floor – a good strike finds its target
- First kick from my hands – feels effortless
- Throwing to the fullbacks – effortless and it arrives in their stride
- Long shot – tipped away for a corner
- Low shot driven in – bounces in front of me but I still hold it comfortably. I can hear the crowd applauding
- Penalty save – I push it away to safety. I can hear the taker cursing

Fullbacks
- First tackle – win the ball and take the player
- Pass down the line – into the stride of the target
- Short ball into midfielder – 'punched' in, a perfect weight for him to turn
- Defending corners – I clear the ball off the line
- Crossing – both first time and after beating my player. Either way I see the striker getting on the end of it and scoring

Centre Halves

- First header – winning it cleanly
- First tackle – take ball cleanly and get the player too
- Pressing my player back – if he's received it, I stand up and prevent the turn, forcing him back
- Clearances – reading the game and just being in the right place at the right time
- Scoring – from a corner or free kick, heading the ball past the keeper

Central Midfielders – Defending

- Tackles – crisp and lets the player know I'm there. Ball falls to a team mate
- Headers – winning every header, even against bigger opponents
- Second ball – first to every one, always in the right place at the right time
- Defending set pieces – I'll run through anything we've worked on in training or seen on video from the other team

Central Midfielders – Attacking

- The first pass – clean and crisp, perfectly weighted
- The second pass – I run through making the second pass perfect, just in case the first one hasn't been
- Receiving the ball from the fullback – turning and passing
- Switching play – receiving from a wide midfielder and switching the ball to the opposite fullback
- Passing to feet – to defenders, midfielders and forwards
- Playing the ball into channels – perfectly weighted passes beating the defenders and into the run of the forward
- Scoring – from free kicks, in the box and outside so wherever the ball drops I'm comfortable to strike it

Wide Midfielders

- Getting a good first touch early in the game
- Receiving the ball from the fullback and playing a short pass inside
- Winning a one-on-one chase down the line to cross a ball in
- Beating your player to get a good cross in
- Attacking the back post and scoring from a cross from the opposite wing
- Cutting inside and getting a shot on target
- Tracking back effortlessly and winning the ball back

Forwards

- Getting the first shot on target
- Scoring from every angle and from just about everywhere within about 30 yards of the goal
- Free kicks – hitting the target and scoring
- Corners – winning headers and picking up second balls to score
- Holding the ball up and playing in midfielders
- Beating defenders one-on-one on the floor
- Winning a flick-on against the centre half

Once you've run through everything from the game itself, think about when the game has finished. What will people be saying as you walk off the pitch? Not just your team mates but also your manager, the referee and supporters. Think about the atmosphere in the dressing room. Do all of this as if it is happening exactly as you'd want it to.

If you play at a level where post-match interviews take place, run through yours. What questions will you be asked? Imagine answering them confidently. Think about what you'll say, who you'll thank and how you'll feel.

WHAT YOU CAN USE IT FOR...

Well, almost anything. Positive mental practice is part of any successful player's general preparation. If you think back to the hows and whys mentioned earlier, it's important to remember that *you can improve specific skills* through proper mental practice. Here are some examples.

- Practising penalties
- Free kicks – the skill and the routine
- Corners
- Finishing
- Heading – attacking and defending
- Passing
- Your performance in the post-match interview
- Tackling
- Even making sure you say the right things to the manager in negotiations

If you would like an additional mental practice technique, try posing the mental rehearsal in your mind and zooming in on a specific detail such as the texture of the ball, the temperature in your mind, or on certain supporters.

Remember: the more adept you can become at this technique, the more you are in control of your performance. The sporting greats such as Ali, Beckham, Wilkinson among many, many others do this naturally, so why not be more like them?

KEY POINTS TO REMEMBER

- Mental practice sends the same messages around the body as actual 'practice'.
- Most people mentally rehearse, but most rehearse things going badly.
- Mental practice should become as much part of your routine as training and eating well.
- Spend a minimum of five minutes on mental practice every day.
- Rehearsing in all the senses is much more powerful than just visualisation.
- For the most successful players, mental practice is a habit.
- Use it for any skill or technique that you want to improve on or off the pitch.

RAISING YOUR MENTAL GAME IMPROVES PERFORMANCE AND CONSISTENCY

James O'Connor is a former Republic of Ireland Under-21 international and, having played at Stoke City and West Bromwich Albion, is now driving the midfield at Championship side Burnley. During Burnley's outstanding run in the first part of the 2006-07 season, James was recognised as a key element in the team's success. He is clear that increased focus on mental fitness has resulted in more consistent and improved performances.

'I've always looked after myself physically,' he said.

'Fitness is a key part of my game so I work hard even during the off-season as well as paying close attention to my diet. I really believe that developing tools to focus your mind is as important as, for example, keeping hydrated. Ultimately if you are relaxed and confident before and during a game you'll play well and if you aren't then you won't. If that's the case, it is important for me to know how to get relaxed and confident, especially before the really key games. That for me is mental fitness.'

Positive mental rehearsal is a key element of James' routine (see Chapter 9). 'I spend five minutes every morning thinking about what I want to happen and, really importantly for me, how I want to feel. Then every Thursday I spend around 30 minutes really relaxing while thinking about the game at the weekend. This routine has helped me to relax and become less anxious about the games. There were times in the past when I'd get so hyped about the game on the Thursday that I was using energy up two days beforehand. Now I can concentrate on being clear on what I need to do and allow myself to really get up for the game just before kickoff.'

The best individual example of the results of this process was a game in the 2006-07 season. James spent more time than he would normally mentally rehearsing both the game and what would happen afterwards. 'I ran through phases of play in my head, how I wanted to feel following my first tackle and other key areas of my game that are part of my routine. I also focused on what would be happening after the game. A good friend of mine had been over from Ireland on trial with Ipswich but had become really ill at a crucial stage. I wanted to be part of the post-match interview on TV so I could give him a mention, and in order to do that I'd need to score or get man of the match.

'I actually did both, and as I was handed the man of the match award I was able to wish my friend all the best for his recovery. That was probably my best game of the season and I'm sure it was down to how clearly I rehearsed what happened during and after the game.'

There is another key element of James' mental practice that has really helped him to focus on making the game as simple as possible. 'During games I focus on "next ball", whether that is a pass, tackle, header or shot. In the past I would sometimes find myself thinking about the result, how I was playing, how I played in the last game and a load of other stuff. Having the trigger of "next ball" just keeps my mind on exactly what I need to be doing.'

James' reflections are a clear indication of the impact of mental fitness. His diet is specially planned, he drinks no alcohol and sleeps well. He has a great support team of family and friends and he trains almost every day, even during the off-season. The only thing that could have been improved was his ability to relax and focus on specific aspects of his game.

When he did that, he was able to take even greater advantage of his physical ability.

CHAPTER 10
RETIRING FROM FOOTBALL

Newcastle's Alan Shearer scores in his testimonial against Celtic at St James' Park, his last match before retirement

SEVEN THINGS YOU MUST DO IF RETIRING FROM FOOTBALL IS DIFFICULT

- You have to find another healthy way to replace the 'needs' that playing football meets. If not, you will meet them in an unhealthy way.
- Create a 'vision of the future', describing a positive version of your life without football. This is especially important if you are a professional, although if playing football at any level has played a key part in your life this will be helpful.

- Adjust your diet to take into account the reduced amount of exercise you are doing. If you put on weight it makes the transition even more difficult.

- Involve other people in the change. Even if you are the type of person who doesn't normally talk about feelings, this is a time when you must. As well as the obvious people like your partner or family, find someone who has been through it and is now happy without football and find out what they did.

- Decide whether to walk away from the game completely or be involved in another capacity. We've known players who have decided to retire in their early thirties and never kicked another ball or watched another game. Similarly we know people who go from player to coach, coach to manager, manager to technical director, technical director to scout. Some people get at least a little of the buzz of playing from being involved in 'banter' and the routine in some other way. For others there is playing, or nothing. There is no general right or wrong in this, only what works best for you.

- Learn something new. Learning creates new pathways in the mind and allows your whole focus to change. So choose something that interests you, but don't limit yourself to something conventional. Whether you learn a new language or take a coaching course, getting a new skill will keep your brain sharp and help rewire it away from being a footballer.

- Do something that gives you some 'closure'. This might be a farewell testimonial or some other special last game or even a farewell party or meal. Often players avoid this because they want to make it easier in the future to come back. If you have made the decision to stop because your body can't carry on or because you have slipped down to such a low standard that you don't want to play any more, then make it public.

HOW FOOTBALL MEETS YOUR NEEDS

If you think about all of the tough choices you've had as a footballer and all of the physical and social sacrifices that you have made, you might wonder why you got involved in the first place.

The truth is that being involved in the game meets some fundamental human needs that we all have.

These needs have been made popular by life coach and practical psychologist Anthony Robbins, and are a powerful model upon which to build tools to take control of your life.

FIGURE 10.1 THE SIX HUMAN NEEDS

The Six Human Needs
Certainty (or security)
Uncertainty (or variety)
Connection (or love)
Significance
Growth
Contribution

Before we look at each need in more detail, here are the headlines of what you need to know about these needs:

- We will meet these needs one way or the other. It isn't a choice.
- Some of the needs conflict with each other. That's why life is so interesting!
- Any activity or behaviour that meets three or more of these needs will become addictive, even if it isn't healthy or pleasant.
- These needs are in every part of our life, not just our work or social life.
- We can do things that meet the first four needs and still be unhappy. The final two needs are called fulfilment needs. We must feel that we are learning and developing and contributing to something to feel truly happy.

UNDERSTANDING YOUR NEEDS

Certainty

We all have a need for some element of routine, security and assurance. At a basic level, we want to know that when we turn the tap on, water will come out and that, when we check our bank balance, there will be money in it. In terms of football, the need is met by the routine provided by meeting times and regularity of training. Many players even introduce their own additional match day routines. If you have ever wondered why one player has to put their left shinpad on before their right, or why another player has to put their shirt on only as they walk on to the pitch, they are unconsciously meeting a need for additional certainty.

Uncertainty

Yes, these two needs directly conflict. If we do things that give us a great feeling of certainty in our lives, we will become bored or restless. This is why people can strive to become accepted at a club and then, as soon as they are, they ask for a transfer. Remember too that, because the same needs apply to every part of our lives, football is a great way to give us more uncertainty because we don't know whether we are going to win or lose, whether we are going to be selected or left out, and so on.

Connection

We all have a need to feel part of some group and linked to other people. Even people who enjoy their own company and like to be seen as an individual often seek to join groups or wear certain clothes. For example, wearing designer clothes is a great way to get connection while still being individual. Connection is perhaps the most obvious need that is met by football. Many people we meet wonder who their friends would be if they had never been involved in the game. It is more than just being part of a team on match day. It is the social aspect and the long-term friendships that are formed.

Significance

There is an ironic conflict between this need and the previous one. We want to feel connected and part of a team, but we don't want to lose our identity. We want to feel that we are a key part of the squad, but also that we're somehow different from the others. Again, because these needs cover every part of our lives, if we aren't getting enough significance through our football, we will seek it in other ways. This can include being unfaithful, causing arguments, doing charity work or anything else that gets significant attention from other people, either for good or bad reasons.

Growth

In order to feel happy and worthwhile we must feel like we are learning new things, developing new skills or abilities or improving ourselves in some other way.

Contribution

Do you give something to a group or to your family? Do you know that people or your team benefit from having you around? This need to add value to some greater good is key to whether we feel happy and fulfilled.

HOW THE NEEDS DICTATE OUR BEHAVIOUR

Have you ever experienced a situation where someone you know has everything they want, then they started to self-destruct? This is the result of human needs playing out at their worst. Everything from drug taking to becoming a member of a gang can be attributed to the six human needs.

More importantly in the context of a player retiring, football meets every single one of the needs, usually at a high level, and therefore is highly addictive. Remember that these needs are not something we try to meet; we just do, one way or the other. This means that when you stop playing, you will replace the unattended needs somehow – even if in unhelpful ways.

CASE STUDY – PROBLEMS WHEN RETIRING FROM AMATEUR FOOTBALL

Mark (not his real name) played football from the age of 12, including school teams, boys' club, and representative football. On leaving school, he went on to play non-league football as well as local football on a Sunday morning.

He was highly committed to his team, training twice a week, and captained several of the teams he played for throughout his career. He also enjoyed the social aspect of the game and usually signed for teams where he knew the management or other players.

At the age of 26 he was accused of assaulting an opponent and, while the case was disproved, he decided to stop playing.

His wife noticed that he was becoming increasingly argumentative, especially at weekends, and was demanding more attention from her. He also began travelling more through his work and spent less time with his family.

While neither Mark nor his wife could really understand what was causing the unrest, a review of the human needs gives a useful insight.

After years of being involved in a sport that met all of his needs at a high level, Mark was getting the significance previously provided by football by creating disagreements. Arguments are a great way of getting connection (or attention) from another person. Travel met the need for variety previously provided by mixed results and team selection.

He eventually started to train with his old team mates and eventually began playing again. As you would expect, the arguments at home stopped and his travel reduced.

CASE STUDY – PROBLEMS WHEN RETIRING FROM PROFESSIONAL FOOTBALL

Steve (again, not his real name) was a professional footballer throughout the 1990s. He played for various clubs in the top flight, including a club 20 miles from where he grew up. He represented England before injury and lack of fitness led to his retirement in his early thirties.

His career had left him financially secure. However, after several months of doing very little other than a few games of golf, his wife became increasingly unhappy. Steve had reorganised their home, taken control of the shopping, spent lots of time socialising and had become more and more unpredictable. He could go from being the life and soul of the party to completely miserable and quite angry in minutes. He also doubted himself much more.

She approached several local football academies to ask if they would consider giving her husband a coaching position. The academies questioned why a millionaire ex-international footballer would want to work in a football academy, especially for free.

A reference back to the human needs provides a useful insight. Steve's need for significance and connection had previously been met strongly by his fans, team mates and other people around his club and international team. When he retired, taking charge in the home and creating more and more opportunities to socialise met these needs. Yet because he wasn't meeting the fulfilment needs (growth and contribution), he was still unhappy and his wife even more so.

While coaching didn't completely replace the feeling of playing on the big stage, he was at least able to feel he was having to think and therefore learn, and was contributing to the careers of young players. He also reduced the amount of time he spent drinking as his need for connection was met during his coaching.

Steve has gone on to manage various local non-league teams.

These case studies highlight one simple fact:

When you retire, you will meet your needs somehow. You must plan how you will replace them in a positive, useful and healthy way or you could end up sabotaging your health, relationship or friendships, or all three.

REPLACE YOUR NEEDS

Here is an exercise to help you work out how football currently meets your needs and how to make sure that, when you retire, you meet these needs in a positive way.

On page 98 is a table to capture your thoughts in. Think about how football meets each need for you. Then, in the next column, describe how you might meet the need if you were going to sabotage yourself after retirement. Finally, think how you could meet this need in a way that is positive and helpful.

We've included an example table to help your thought process.

TABLE 10.1 EXAMPLE TABLE OF NEEDS

Need	How football meets this need	A negative way this need could be met	A positive way to meet this need
Certainty	The routine of training, match day	Eating – know I'll feel full afterwards; also drinking – I know I'll get drunk	Hard exercise for a short time three times a week
Uncertainty	Not knowing whether we'll win or lose or whether I'll be selected or not	Cheating on my partner and running the risk of getting caught	Taking up another sport such as golf or getting involved in coaching or managing another team
Connection	The team bond plus the social side of the club	Regularly going out drinking or hanging around with other unsociable groups	More regular contact with family members or close friends

RETIRING FROM FOOTBALL 97

Need	How football meets this need	A negative way this need could be met	A positive way to meet this need
Significance	Being able to talk about playing football and the team, and the individual significance during games	Arguing with my wife or close family	Building close ties with a community group or becoming a key member of some other group
Growth	Learning new aspects of the game or developing technically, tactically or physically	Any obsessive learning or growth	Taking a coaching course
Contribution	Helping young players develop and helping the team to victory	Sharing too many stories of how good I used to be	Coaching, managing or sponsoring a local club or junior team

TABLE 10.2 YOUR OWN TABLE OF NEEDS

Now complete your own…

Need	How football meets this need	A negative way this need could be met	A positive way to meet this need
Certainty			
Uncertainty			
Connection			

Significance		
Growth		
Contribution		

SIX HUMAN NEEDS SUMMARY

When you retire you will feel that there is something missing, but the big challenge is that most of the problem behaviours that come as a result of the human needs are unconscious. In other words, you do them without thinking or realising.

Doing the exercise on the previous pages and even just knowing about the needs puts you back in charge of your life after football.

YOUR FUTURE HISTORY

Design Your Life Exercise

Imagine you could fast-forward twelve months from now. Imagine your life was exactly as you would want it to be. What would that perfect life be?

- Think about how you will be physically and mentally.
- What will your relationships be like?
- If you aren't already financially secure, how will you be earning your money?
- If you are financially secure, how will you be spending your time?
- What will your social life be like?
- How will you be meeting your human needs in a positive, healthy way?
- What will people around you be saying about you?
- Most importantly, how will you be feeling?

Create this ideal life in as much detail as possible. It doesn't matter whether you write or draw it, but it is useful to have it recorded somewhere so you can look at it in the future to see how much of it has come true.

Once you have designed your future, think about the following questions.

- Imagine that we could absolutely guarantee that this was going to be your life in twelve months' time, provided you took some small action to support it in coming true. What would be the first small steps you would take?
- Now imagine that there was a £1 million prize on offer. If all you had to do to win this prize was to create the life you've just described, what plan would you put in place to make sure you achieved it?

For the record, £1 million isn't on offer, but you would be surprised at the number of people who do this exercise and somehow manage to achieve the financial goals they set themselves.

We just want to take the time to remind you of something that has been a key underpinning factor in the exercises throughout this book, just in case you have not managed to read it all (you should, by the way: it's really quite good!).

Your brain is designed in such a way that it will do its best to follow any command it is given. Therefore, if you design a detailed future history, your brain will search for a way to make sure that this happens, even without you realising.

By designing a future exactly as you would want it, even just on a small piece of paper, you dramatically increase the chances of this outlook coming true.

There is also an added bonus. While the brain is an amazing piece of equipment, remember that it does not differentiate between what is real and what is strongly imagined. In this respect, having a future history in itself makes you happier and more fulfilled, because the brain automatically produces feel-good chemicals as if it has already happened.

- What happens if you don't design your life after football? You cannot achieve your goals – simply because you have not set any.
- You will be more prone to being unhappy and especially feeling listless.
- You are less likely to keep yourself fit and healthy. Why would you? You haven't got any reason to.
- People who set themselves targets in this way are popularly believed to be financially better off than those who don't.
- Life will pass you by.

A SUMMARY OF WORKING WITH RETIRING FOOTBALLERS

This area of our work is one that we're incredibly passionate about, yet it's the one in which we've found it most difficult to have an influence.

Let's use a retiring professional as an example. These broadly fall into one of two categories. First you have the player who has played further down the leagues all of their lives. Perhaps they've earned enough to have a decent lifestyle, but certainly are not wealthy. This player is likely to be ending their playing career in their mid- to late thirties so have fifty to sixty years of life left.

They may get a retirement payout from the PFA or similar players' union, but that will quickly be used up maintaining their home and car. Keep in mind that the player and his family will have got used to, at the very least, a decent standard of living. How will the player maintain this when they are unlikely to have any other skill or profession to fall back on? He may decide to go into coaching or do some media work, but these fields are surprisingly low paid, unless you are at the very top end – a bit like playing football actually.

On top of that, the player does not have the routine of training or games. Nor does he get the attention that he once did from supporters, and even some friends and family members are less interested generally in how things are.

The second category of player also faces the challenges of life without the certainty of daily training and a match or two a week. But these players have other, slightly different, challenges. Most people would think that being a top-level professional who has already made all the money they could ever need would leave you with no problems following retirement. While I'm sure these players would not swap their career for anything, what do you do for the rest of your life when you don't have to do anything? How do you get motivated? Also, how do you replace the buzz that comes from playing at the very highest level of the game? How do you replace the attention and, in some cases, adulation that comes from being in that position? Retirement from this position certainly leaves some significant gaps to fill in life.

We believe there are some significant holes in the support given to players in this position. Many need help in developing practical skills, and that kind of assistance is, to some degree, there. More importantly, many need coaching and support in adjusting to their new lives and frankly many do not even realise that this support is available.

This might be interesting reading for those of you playing for pleasure, but not directly relevant. You must accept though that if you are serious about your football, even if it is just in a Sunday league, you must find something else that provides the same buzz and excitement for you in some other positive way. The real beauty of football is that, whether you are playing or managing on your local council pitch or at your national stadium for your national team, the same feelings are generated and the same needs are met. And when it has gone, the same gaps must be plugged.

KEY POINTS TO REMEMBER

- If you feel that retirement is something natural and that you do not need to work on any replacement of human needs, this means one of two things:
  a) You are very lucky, or
  b) You are fulfilling your needs somehow, without realising.
  In fact, if it is a), then it is because b) is happening.
- The key thing to remember, as we've repeated throughout the chapter, is that human needs are not something we choose to meet. We will meet them somehow. Our choice, and the area of focus, must be how we meet them.

THE SCOUT'S VIEW

Winners want to gain respect

Ralf Wright made his name as an uncompromising defender
in non-league football in the northeast of England before
going on to play for Bolton, Southport, New York Cosmos and
Fort Lauderdale Strikers.

Among his many proud achievements, Wright is one of
the few players who prevented Pelé from scoring each time
he played against him.

He now works as a scout for Manchester City. Having
joined the club as part of Stuart Pearce's backroom staff,
he now supports Sven-Göran Eriksson as the senior scout in
the northeast.

Commenting on his own playing experiences, he
highlights a key mental driver. 'I always wanted to gain the
respect of my opponents. Even towards the end of my career
it was always easy for me because I wanted to give
everything. It's the only way I knew how to play.

'In my early days one manager told me that he was
always happy if my opponent kicked me early in the game,
because it really spurred me into action. I would become a
different, much more physical player. If players can learn to
create this spur themselves it is incredibly useful.'

This desire and will to win is something that Ralf looks
for when he is scouting.

'I look for players that have a resilience and persistence
to impose themselves on their opponents. If they try to beat
their man and it doesn't work, will they keep trying
something else until they are successful? All too often, I see

players who take the easy option. For example, I watch a current international winger playing regularly. I just do not see what he does that gets him into the international team. For me a good attacking wide midfield will regularly beat the fullback and put a cross in. It is not enough just to stay wide and pass the ball into the central midfielders. This is the easy option for the individual but adds too little to the team.'

He adds that his playing days taught him a lot about the difference between those players with real resilience and those that could easily be put off their game.

'I was a very physical player. I was not hugely skilful, but I was happiest stopping those that were skilful from having an effect on the game. Some players could be talked out of playing well; even telling them how hard you were going to tackle them would see them going out of their way to avoid you. With others, they would disappear after they had been on the receiving end of a strong challenge. The rest were more of a concern. I remember playing in Columbia against a big physical centre forward, so I decided to hit him as hard as I could. When I did, he smiled and came back for more. I knew then I was really in a game.'

While the game is not as physical as it used to be, the same principles still apply.

'I watched a Premiership game last night and after one strong tackle, one of the game's key creative players changed position. It left his team with less in the way of attacking options and the opposition had a much easier time defensively. It frustrates me to see a player with so much ability allowing themselves to be bullied out of a game so easily. I would have expected it to take much more than one tackle.'

When questioned about whether this commitment decreases over time, Ralf is clear in his beliefs.

'The desire to give everything is one of the last things to go. In the past I have played with greats like Roger Hunt and Chris Lawler who played at the very top of football and they went out and gave their all in every game, even when their legs were starting to go.'

He continued: 'I left New York Cosmos the season before Pelé joined, which was slightly disappointing, but I had the pleasure of playing against him several times. Anyone that thinks that players like Pelé, Franz Beckenbauer, Geoff Hurst and Peter Bonetti who went to America in that period just went for the money and the sun are mistaken. Pelé was all over the pitch. One minute he would be clearing the ball off his own goal line and the next he would be scoring at the other end. When you have commitment like this, mixed with undoubted quality (Pelé once nutmegged me and patted me on the head as he went past), that is when you get high performance.'

He added: 'Players who don't have this real desire to gain respect from their opponents must develop mental strength in this area. You cannot have a career these days without 100 per cent commitment. At the top level, players are not just talented footballers, they are real athletes. You have to be prepared to go the extra mile to compete with and get the better of your opponents. If you have got the desire, it will stay with you until you retire.'

Wright's thoughts on retirement reflect the tools and techniques in this chapter.

'When you stop playing, it leaves a huge gap. I kept going as long as I possibly could because I did not know what I would do without it. Some players take up golf, or go into coaching, but ultimately you must find something that replaces the intense feelings and of course the routine that you get from playing.' He continues: 'I worry about certain players as they retire. I think it is too easy to start drinking, or doing other things that are destructive. Most players need some support to plug this gap and plan for the rest of their lives. You are a long time retired. I know that as much as any others and I'm really lucky to still be involved in the game that I love.'

CHAPTER 11

AT THE END OF THE DAY

Kevin Phillips and team mates celebrate his last-minute winner for West Bromwich Albion in a Football League Championship game

In the classic movie *Any Given Sunday* Al Pacino gives a motivational half-time speech to his struggling American football team. 'Life, like football, is a game of inches,' he tells them, 'and the inches you need are all around you.'

We believe this to be true. Often the difference between winning and losing a football match is a matter of hundredths of a second, the width of a goal post or half a yard of pace.

If the gap between success and failure is that small, then surely any player, manager or coach will do whatever they can to gain any advantage? Certainly some do. The first time we worked with Craig Armstrong, he told us that anything that gives him even a 1 per cent lift, he would do.

That is why we wrote this book. We want every serious footballer to have at their fingertips the tools and techniques to help them realise their potential. When we use the word 'realise', we mean it in both senses. 'Realise' in terms of understanding that you have the ability to develop every aspect of your game and become more successful and consistent. 'Realise' too in terms of fulfilling that potential. Doing this means taking some action and, in modern football, it means taking action in new and innovative ways.

Of course, not everyone in football is so forward thinking and focused on doing what it takes. There is scepticism and fear about the application of psychological techniques, but this attitude is changing. Our client base has grown significantly, with more players, managers and even chairmen embracing the techniques in this book.

This is helped by an increased acceptance of practical psychologies such as Neuro-Linguistic Programming (NLP). While we have some concerns about the way some of the tools associated with NLP are applied, anything that helps players get the most from their careers, whether that is at a recreational level or professionally, has got to be a good thing.

WHERE IS THE PROOF?

While writing this book, we've had an interesting dilemma. How do we balance the need to keep the book practical enough for its target audience while acknowledging that some readers, in particular the sceptics mentioned above and those from a more traditional sports psychology background, will be looking for more evidence that these tools work?

In the end the decision was easy. This book is for everyday people who just happen to be involved in football. Our experience is that you don't really want or need to know the formal research. If you are assured that these tools work for other people, and that they are likely to work for you, you will give them a go and see what happens.

If you have got this far through the book having read most or all of it, let us congratulate you. Research shows that many people who buy books to improve their performance never read past the first chapter. Of course, this also means that, when you apply what you have read and do the exercises, you are giving yourself an advantage.

As we've mentioned earlier in the book, we strongly believe that the gaps in the technical, tactical and physical aspects of football are closing. The advantage is, even more than ever, in the mind.

So the proof is ultimately in the results. If you use the tools, especially as part of your match preparation routine, you will without doubt become your own walking, talking case study of evidence. To state the obvious, if you don't try them, they definitely will not work for you.

PERFORMANCE AND POTENTIAL

There is an equation that is often used in acting and the arts to describe the link between performance and potential:

$$P = p - i$$

In this equation, P is your performance level – how well you are playing. The second 'p' is your potential – in other words, all the skills, abilities, technical, tactical and physical awareness you have. Finally, 'i' is interference. In football this can be physical if you are carrying an injury, but in most cases this interference is the mental intrusion that we cause ourselves. It is our unhelpful states, our critical internal dialogue, the pressure that we create because of the way the manager or the crowd is reacting to us.

When you can manage your interference, then you can really realise your potential.

FINAL WORDS

If you start competitive football at eight years old, then retire when you are thirty-eight, you are likely to have fifty to sixty years of your life without playing the beautiful game. Because of this we urge you to do two things.

- The first is to play for as long as your body allows. We all have phases where we wonder why we play, but they will pass. If you get into your forties and wish you had played more, there is little you can do. This also applies to any well-paid professionals reading this. You must look after your financial interests, but please do consider whether moving clubs and playing regularly will lead to fewer regrets.
- The second is to use the information in this book in the other fifty years of your life. You can apply every tool, from anchoring to relaxation techniques and from mental rehearsal to controlling fear and anger, in every other area of life, including your family, your career outside of football, your health and your finances.

Remember that life is not about the number of breaths that we take, but the number of moments that take our breath away.

Enjoy your football.

As a manager, Sir Bobby Robson won honours wih Ipswich Town, PSV Eindhoven, FC Porto and Barcelona, as well as managing other top clubs and the England team

PART 3: LEADERSHIP AND SUPPORT ROLES

CHAPTER 12

A GUIDE FOR MANAGERS, COACHES AND CAPTAINS

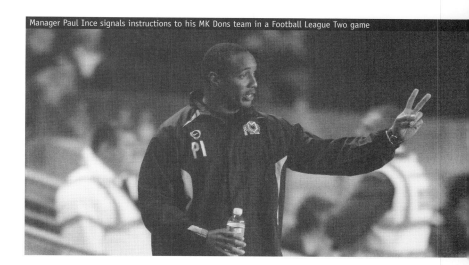

Manager Paul Ince signals instructions to his MK Dons team in a Football League Two game

HOW TO MOTIVATE, INSPIRE, AND GET MORE RESPECT AND BETTER RESULTS

This chapter has been written especially for you if:

- You want to motivate your players to get even better results;
- You want your players to do what you ask of them more of the time;
- You want more respect or buy-in to your ideas;
- You want to get more from your players, especially if you have limited resources;
- You constantly need to have a go at the players around you and are thinking 'there must be another way'.

Some extra things we want you to know:

- The same principles apply to the top end of the game and to the grass roots. We have helped coaches at every level using these principles and techniques.
- If you are a player or are involved in the game in some other way, it is still worth reading this section. You'll find some useful ideas for getting people around you more motivated during training and matches. You will also increase your chances of being made captain in the future.
- Just like the other chapters in this book, the principles are based on hard research. We have purposely avoided detailing this research, but if you are the type of person who likes more theory, research and evidence then please feel free to get stuck into the reading list at the end of the book.

LEADING PEOPLE IN FOOTBALL

A huge amount of research has been done over the years into what people in various walks of life want from the people who lead and manage them. Most people want their leaders to be:

- Honest
- Forward-looking
- Capable
- Inspiring

A Quick Questionnaire

Answer the following questions using the 1–6 scale (1 being low or not at all and 6 being high or all the time).

When a player asks your opinion on how well they played, how often do you give them a balanced honest view?

1   2   3   4   5   6

How well do the players around you know your views on how the game should be played?

1   2   3   4   5   6

How well developed is your vision of the future for your team or club?

1   2   3   4   5   6

Do you have clear goals for this season and for next?

1   2   3   4   5   6

How often do people comment on your ability to do your job in your club?

1   2   3   4   5   6

How often do you do any development activities (including attending a course, reading a book or watching a game specifically to pick up new tips or ideas)?

1   2   3   4   5   6

How many different positive ways do you use to enthuse and motivate the players in your club?

1   2   3   4   5   6

How many of your players do you think would describe you as 'inspirational'?

1   2   3   4   5   6

Now calculate your score by adding up your responses to the questions. The maximum score is 48 and the minimum is 8.

Think about the results and use the following questions to form actions that will improve your leadership standing.

- What are you already very good at? How can you do even more of this?
- What can you do to take each of the scores one point higher up the scale?
- Which areas must you take immediate action on?

DEMONSTRATING HONESTY

Let us start by defining honesty. Does it mean you have got to give away all of your secrets? No. Does it mean that when a player's confidence is rock bottom you tell them again exactly how terribly they are playing? Preferably not.

In a football context, honesty means that players know where they stand, know what they can expect of you and what you expect of them. It means you do what you say whenever possible and when it is not, you say why.

Creating A Team Charter

One of the quickest and easiest ways to build a sense of trust and transparency in the dressing room is to develop a team charter. This helps the players know what to expect from you and each other. If you are someone who struggles to demand discipline from players, either because of your personality or the level of football you are at, this is a perfect way to get the players to self-manage more.

Get your players to identify a team that they believe is performing outstandingly well and that clearly works hard for each other and has great team spirit.

Group your squad into three or four smaller teams. Get them to identify five to eight characteristics that this high performance team has. These must be more about the behaviours that the team demonstrates, rather than skills or ability.

Collate the characteristics that your team have come up with on a flipchart or whiteboard. Get the team to vote on the most important eight out of the list they have come up with. What you have now is a list of the eight most important characteristics or behaviours of a high performing team, as defined by your team.

Now get each player and member of the coaching team to physically sign this list.

These behaviours should be used to manage your squad. When the charter is being compiled you do have the power to reject any item, but it is vital that you can clearly say why you are doing this. By regularly reminding your players of the charter, you are making clear what you expect of them and in fact what they expect of each other. It is much more difficult for a player to argue against any part of this charter when they have helped design it.

Giving Them the News

> 'A great coach once told me that leadership started with telling people the truth – no better and no worse. It seems to be a common trait of many of the coaches and managers that we come across that they would rather not have a conversation at all than have a difficult one.' Richard

Our experience shows that this is the worst thing you can do in most situations. We recently spoke to a client who was stripped of the club captaincy with no explanation.

'I had been out injured for a few games and came back into the team as soon as I was fit. We had signed a new central defensive partner for me and it was his first game for the club too. Just as we were getting ready to go out the manager threw him the captain's armband. He never said anything to me. I was upset at losing the captaincy but I was even angrier that the manager didn't have the guts or the respect to speak to me and tell me why. At that moment I decided to leave the club.'

A few months later this player joined a new club for a seven-figure fee and was quickly installed as club captain.

So the learning point is simple – if there is a conversation to be had, then have it.

Here are three key points to help you make these conversations as positive as possible.

● Describe the situation as it is – no better and no worse.
● Have the conversation at the right time. Do not leave it too long and never do it just before a game.

- Be clear on what you are going to say before you have the conversation and make sure you are consistent with your message. Contradicting yourself will ruin your credibility.

By having these honest and clear conversations with players, you are giving them more of a sense of certainty about where they stand with you. They will not always like you, nor will they always agree. But they will respect you for having the conversation with them, rather than randomly dropping them or making sweeping statements about who is playing well or who is playing badly.

One final thought. Being honest includes telling players when they have played well. Please remember to do this. If you tell a player specifically what they have done well, you are increasing the chances of them doing it again. This probably sounds obvious but in a recent straw poll survey we carried out with professional and semi-professional players, only about 10 per cent could remember the last time their manager specifically told them what they had done well.

BEING FORWARD-LOOKING

Being forward-looking is, as you would expect, about focusing on the future rather than the past. While some analysis of what has worked and what hasn't is useful, what really counts is what happens in the next game and into the future.

Think about how much time you spend with your players talking about what has happened, and what must happen. Have you got the balance right?

Create A Vision Of The Future

This tool will be used differently depending on the level of football you are at and whether you are a player, coach or captain. The basics of the approach remain the same, however; you might just need to adjust the level of detail or the timescale.

- Decide how far into the future you would like to create your vision for. For most people, we'd recommend somewhere around 12 to 18 months as being the most useful.
- Now imagine you can fast-forward to this time and that your team has developed in exactly the way you would want it to. Write down everything that you can think of that would be different. Use the following questions as prompts. The purpose is to create a mental picture of exactly how you want things to be at this point in the future.
  - How will the team be playing?
  - What will you be saying to the players?
  - What will they be saying to each other and how will they be as a team?
  - What results will the team be getting, where will you be in the league and what do you want other people to be saying about you?
  - How will the squad and the players in it have developed?
  - If appropriate, where will the club, team or players be financially?
- Share this vision with the team. Let them know the part they play in making this vision become a reality. Also let them know what you are going to be doing to make sure this vision happens.

● If you find this useful, we would recommend using this vision as the basis of a plan for the development of your team or club. What are the steps that you need to take over the coming months to ensure that this vision is achieved?

Creating Shared Aims

We firmly believe that if you play an influential role in a team at any level, you should have clear aims for that team. Whereas once it was enough for players just to turn up and play, these days even Sunday league teams know what league position is required to make the season a success and what would not be acceptable.

While this is a step forward, team aims are much more likely to be achieved if they are just that: aims created by the whole team. Use the form below to collect the shared aims from your team.

TABLE 12.1 CREATING TEAM AIMS

In terms of league and cup results, what would make the season a highly successful one?
What are your minimum expectations for the end of the season for the team?

What would make this season highly successful for you personally?

Who else will contribute to this season being highly successful? How will they contribute?

Once you have got answers to these questions from all of your players, collate them and create an overall team goal for minimum and maximum achievement, based on the overall views of the squad.

We would also recommend that you share your players' individual targets with the other members of the squad. This again creates more of a shared ownership throughout the squad.

The balance between the forward-looking and backward-looking in football is something that fascinates us. Let us state the most obvious thing in this book so far: you cannot change the result of a game that has already been played.

BEING CAPABLE

This is perhaps the most important quality to describe. It also becomes the hardest to maintain the longer you are in the game. Your management and leadership style is likely to be a combination of three main influences: previous managers and coaches you have played under; the managers you most enjoyed playing under; and outside factors such as training courses or experience you have of managing or leading outside of football.

In the past ten years there have been huge changes at every level of the game. At the top level, money and celebrity are king. Even at the grass roots of the game, players get notoriety through social networking or club websites, while there is an ever-decreasing pool of players to choose from because of changes in working patterns and a much greater choice of activities.

All this means you must keep your capabilities up to date. Like any good workman, your tools must be sharp. Here are our key 'dos and don'ts' for ensuring you keep your skills, knowledge and ability up to date.

Dos

- Read books by the best in the business. Most successful coaches, managers and leaders bring out a biography or some 'how to' book. Take the best of their suggestions and add them to your 'toolkit'.

- If you are not a big reader, look for DVDs, CDs or even movies that will expand your horizons. *Any Given Sunday* is just one of the many films with an outstanding motivational speech as well as many other useful learning points for any leader.

- Take your coaching qualifications. While some experienced people see the modern badges as a means to an end, you are highly unlikely to go through the whole process without picking up any new tools and techniques. Perhaps even more importantly than the course itself, you will get to see a range of other coaches in action, all with their own style and approach.

- Expand your horizons beyond your team. If you coach in the professional game, make some connections with coaches abroad. Visit other clubs with very different styles and learn from them. If you are lower down in the footballing pyramid, make a similar connection with other clubs in a similar league to you and do the same.

- Expand your horizons beyond your sport. For example, if you are a club captain, spend some time finding out more about how captains in other sports influence the players in their team, in particular sports such as rugby and basketball where captains have an even greater role on and off the pitch. Similarly, as a manager, what could you learn from successful coaches in other sports or even business?

Don'ts

- Constantly refer back to previous successes. Winning the league ten years ago might have been the foundation that got you to where you are now, but it certainly does not guarantee success or even respect now.

- Talk about previous players as if they were heroes that can't be matched. If you do this, the chances are your suggestion will come true and current players will never reach these heights.

- Rest on your laurels and keep doing the same things season after season. It's fair to say that players at most levels are now fitter than they were ten years ago. It is probably also fair to say that at most levels the players are less technically able. So if that is the case, anyone who is still using training techniques from ten years ago is probably concentrating on the wrong areas.

- Regularly use the line 'when I was playing I would have…'. Even if it is true that you would have scored that goal, made that tackle or pulled off that save, this is not coaching. Telling your players how good you were does not help them get any better.

- Dismiss anything that is 'new' or 'modern' as a fad, a 'waste of time' or 'rubbish' (at least not until you have tried it). As we write this book, we do not think that the modern coaching qualifications are perfect by a long chalk, and we hope that even by the time you have read this book they will have improved dramatically. It is notable though that the coaches and managers at the top of the professional game have all taken their coaching badges and say that they have benefited from them. The old school of manager often dismisses them; however, a quick glance at who is successful in the modern game tells a story.

The chances are that somewhere in the dim and distant past, managers dismissed the offside law as some modern fad that would pass, probably because 'it will never catch on'.

We have no doubt that these managers will have been left behind very, very quickly. The one certainty in football is that it will change. Players move on, clubs get promoted or relegated, even laws and leagues change. You have a choice: stay ahead of, or at least in line with, the change, or get swallowed up by it.

One thing is for sure – the capabilities you have today as a leader are what count, not what you had as a player or manager five years ago.

BEING INSPIRING

Here is how the *Encarta World English Dictionary* defines the word 'inspire':

1 Stimulate somebody to do something: to encourage somebody into greater effort, enthusiasm, or creativity.
2 Provoke particular feeling: to arouse a particular feeling in somebody.
3 Cause creative activity: to stimulate somebody to do something, especially creative or artistic work.
4 Physiology – breathe in: to inhale air or a gas into the lungs.

Is this enough to convince you that you must be inspiring?

How about some things that are not included in the definitions above? Inspiring definitely does not involve belittling players, running them so hard in training that they are sick, dropping them or, as we suggested in the previous section, repeatedly telling them how good you or other players are.

This might seem obvious, but we have seen managers and coaches at all levels try these strategies and similar ones and label them as motivation or inspiration.

What Inspires You?

Think of a time in the past when someone truly inspired you. Even if this takes time, think about a specific occasion when you felt highly enthusiastic and were most inspired to take action. Write in the space on page 131 what the person did that inspired you.

Now think about the kinds of words that they used and how they used their voice. Describe that in as much detail as you can remember in the space below.

Reflect now on how often you demonstrate the behaviours that you have described above. Are you demonstrating them often enough?

Finally, write in the space below as many situations as you can when you believe it will be useful to be more inspirational.

Typical responses to the questions about what makes someone inspiring are:

- Goes the extra mile – does more than they have to
- Always full of energy
- Always positive
- Gets people going with rousing speeches
- Has overcome great hardship
- Always seems to know the right thing to say and do
- Supportive
- Gets the best out of everyone

BONUS EXERCISE

Martin Luther King's 'I Have A Dream' speech is widely acknowledged as being one of the most inspirational speeches of all time. It can be bought and downloaded from the internet for just a few pounds.

Listen to the speech, in particular the last seven minutes, and write down what makes this speech so inspirational. Focus on the words King uses as well as how he delivers them.

Review all the elements that you think make this speech inspirational and think about how you might be able to apply these when you need to speak to your team.

Being inspiring is a highly underrated quality in football. It is about getting more from your players, creating confidence and passion. When you feel that a game or even season is against you, the ability to inspire can be the difference between a draw and a defeat, or relegation and staying in the division.

If you have done the exercises above, you already have all of the tools and techniques you need to become a more inspiring leader. However, you must use them. For some people charisma and passion come easy; however, for the rest it's something that must be practised.

LEADERSHIP IN FOOTBALL
– A SUMMARY

If you do a quick search in any online bookshop you will find literally hundreds of books about leadership. Over the years there have been thousands of research papers and surveys and hundreds of examples of leadership development making a huge difference in every walk of life from communities to large organisations – and, of course, in sport.

Yet a review of football coaching qualifications from grass roots up to the professional badges shows a big hole when it comes to leadership.

> *'People can't be managed. Inventories can be managed. People must be led.'* H. Ross Perot, billionaire and former US politician

This quote highlights the key difference between leading and managing. Managing in football is all about tactics, team selection, formation, transfer strategy, training plans and all of the other process-related activities that go into making a team successful. However, one common strand runs through all of these activities: people. You must have the players on board to make any of these things happen.

Leadership in football is about getting people to do what you want and need them to, and them doing it because they want to. It is about how you get the extra 5 per cent out of a player that will make the difference in the result of the game. It is about getting a player to do a great job for you in an unfamiliar position and being happy about it.

At one time it was enough to tell a player or even another coach what to do; they would do it because you were in a position of authority. These days they must feel compelled to do it. At the lower end of football, people can move around as they please or stop playing altogether. At the top end, players' profiles and financial security means that they need something other than 'just because'.

Here's a reminder of what people want their leaders to be:

- Honest
- Forward-looking
- Capable
- Inspiring

Great managers do these things naturally, but the capacity to lead can be learned. We're sure that Jose Mourinho has not always had all of his teams 100 per cent behind him, yet one of the most outstanding qualities of his successful spell at Chelsea was the absolute commitment he had from the players.

Remember that these players are superstars in their own right. Players like Didier Drogba, Claude Makelele and Petr Cech had already proven themselves at the very highest level of the game and worked with some of the best coaches in the world. Yet even they had more of a bond with their manager and more of a team spirit than many best friends who have played together for years. Leaders can create that spirit in a way that other managers, coaches or captains can't.

KEY POINTS TO REMEMBER

- Winning in football is a matter of tiny advantages. Developing your ability to lead will give your team these advantages.
- We also strongly believe that leadership can be developed, and in football in particular it must be developed.
- The days when players were happy to be managed are long gone. It just does not work like that any more at any level. You will get more from your players when they want to play for you. Becoming a leader in football will allow you to generate that commitment much more easily.

THE HIDDEN MENTAL PRESSURES OF COMPETITIVE FOOTBALL

Paul McHugh is a UEFA 'A' licensed coach who has first-hand experience of the need for mental fitness in players of all ages. Having worked at several professional clubs including Newcastle United and Hartlepool, he has seen the practical issues faced by players at every age.

'People think that the mental side of the game is just about preparation before games,' said Paul. 'That is massively important but it's just a fraction of what players have to deal with.'

When asked how important the development of a player's mentality is, Paul immediately describes numerous situations that any elite player reading this book will have faced, or will face at some point in their career.

'Imagine going on your first tour with your team. I was recently asked to go to Italy with a Premiership club's Under-11 academy team. The trip was brilliantly organised yet you can imagine that there were several boys who missed home so much. This could develop their mental toughness or it could switch them off from football altogether. If coaches can't support the boys in situations like this, not only will it be detrimental to their performances, it could literally lose them from the game for good.

'Then there are all the decisions that young players have to make. Should they go out with their mates or stay in and rest? They are being asked to play for their academy, their boys' club, their county, district and school teams, and each of these will say their games are the most important. How do we help them develop the decision-making strategies to make considered choices? Remember: we're talking about kids of 11 to 16 here. Then there's their education to consider: where does that fit in?

'Think too of the older players who are looking to secure professional contracts. In their eyes, their whole life balances on a handful of games. They are playing in a team sport, yet are often competing against their team mates. For people in the game, this is what we deal with on a day-today basis. Yet few clubs provide the resources for players and coaches to deal with these pressures effectively. This has to change to help our young players.'

These 'hidden pressures' away from the day to day of football continue throughout a player's career.

Paul continues: 'As players get older, there are choices to be made about drinking, drugs and partners. While everyone faces this, the pressure is even greater on professional footballers because of their financial status and the fact that essentially their body is their tool. Then imagine having a boss that gave you your first contract, gave you your debut, works with you after training and supports your development for the first four years of your professional career. All of a sudden he leaves for whatever reason. A new manager or coach comes in and leaves you out of the team. In a situation that you've never had to deal with before, who supports you? Then there are the financial challenges. Most people outside of the game would be surprised how relatively little players earn outside of the Premiership. Even in the Championship, players may earn the equivalent of a senior manager's salary in a large company, but that is only going to last ten years maximum. So you should save and invest. Yet everyone around you is buying flash cars and watches and you are always expected to pay when you're out with friends or family who have "normal" jobs.

'I could go on and on about all the reasons why players and coaches should have more support in their understanding of mentality and how to develop the number one skill for a successful career in football, mental toughness. Without mental toughness, you've no chance, yet the only way we develop it is by piling on the pressure and seeing who cracks. There must be a better way.

'Having players build routines from an early age does help, providing they aren't so reliant on these routines that they go to pieces if they can't complete them. I also encourage players to think for themselves as much as possible from an early age. We need to help players develop mentally so they can perform physically. To do that, coaches need to develop themselves as much as possible. I even went on some specialist communication and motivation courses run for senior business people to see what I could take from them and apply to my teams. Things like this have really helped; for instance I've applied a load of these techniques when coaching goalkeepers.

'Another key time for players is retirement. Who supports them when they aren't going to play any more? Who helps a player to decide whether to go into the unstable and often low-paid world of coaching or the media or to study for new skills? It's not just about earning money. I've had experience of players who have played at the top offering to work with me for free just to get out of the house because they actually miss the day-to-day routine of going in to train. Again, these are all areas that players should be supported in.'

For anyone involved in the game, Paul McHugh's observations will be all too familiar. That makes it even more important if you are a coach, parent or manager that you use the tools and techniques in this book to support the development of your young players.

CHAPTER 13
A GUIDE FOR PARENTS

Kids' football is about having fun

As a parent you have a vital role in your child's footballing career. You, as much as their ability, dictate whether this is 'for fun' or 'something serious'. We can honestly say that we know many, many more people who say their parents stopped them from going on to play football at a high standard than those who credit their parents with their success.

These are, of course, just our thoughts and you must, as always, support your child as you see fit. But we urge you to follow the first point in the list of key considerations below, if nothing else.

KEY CONSIDERATIONS FOR SUPPORTIVE PARENTS

- It is your child's game. They are playing football for themselves first and foremost. You cannot play it for them and they will not do it they way you want. Help them to enjoy it anyway and guide them to be the best they can, not the best you could have been.

- In most cases you will not be your child's coach. Therefore let their coach do their job, even if it is not how you would coach.

- Consider taking the Football Association's online psychology level 1 course: it's full of useful information for parents.

- Always set a good example on the sidelines and remember that your child will feed from your state (if you have not read the chapter on state in this book, go back and do so now.) If you are over-anxious, aggressive or overly focused on winning, you are an additional pressure to your child.

Understand why children play football.
- Up to the ages of eight or nine, it is just about running around.
- From nine to fourteen, it's about social interaction.
- After the age of fourteen it begins to be about status and competition.
- Shouting and screaming at a seven-year-old because they are not playing well or their team is losing is neither good coaching nor good parenting.

- Focus at least as much on what your child did well in the game as what they could improve on. Many parents just talk about the bad things and never say what the child should be doing instead.

- Have you ever asked your child whether they want you there this week? Maybe you should. Some parents are there too much and some too little, but guess what? It is not you that knows what is too much or little – it is them!

- If you are the coach of your child's team, make sure you have a team charter and that everyone is clear on your selection policy. Keep everything fair, objective and clear. Take the pressure off you and your child.

COMMITMENT UNDERPINS EVERYTHING – THE VIEW FROM A LIVERPOOL FC COACH

David Platt (no relation to the ex-Aston Villa and England midfielder) is well qualified to talk about the importance of mental fitness in the development of young footballers.

As well as being one of the brightest young coaches at Liverpool FC's famous and highly successful youth academy, he has a degree in sports science, a postgraduate advanced certificate in science and football, and a masters degree in sport psychology from John Moores University.

'The mental side of the game is the most important part as it underpins everything else,' he said. 'For example, you must have commitment, motivation and passion in order to develop the technical, tactical and physical aspects of your performance. 'You see the difference after training finishes at every professional club. Those players that really progress do the extra finishing, heading or even spend time with coaches to work on positioning, shape or other tactical aspects. To make this work you've got to be able to focus, have confidence in yourself and your coach and have the ability to reflect on what you learn. These are all mental skills that in themselves can be developed. Players who don't do any of this rarely progress.'

For David, mental development is not just about 'doing extra': it's about dealing with the day-to-day pressures of playing professional football. 'It's a job that is full of routine, pressure, criticism, dips in form and, even at the lower levels, pressure from the media. If a player wants to make the most of their potential, they must improve at a faster rate than the players around them. They must reflect and learn from every game, as well as being able to handle stuff from outside the game. Remember that decision-making is a mental skill. If you are making bad choices about your lifestyle, the friends or partners you choose or your health and fitness, get someone to help you make better choices.

'We suggest that players should set aims every day. For example, if a player has been told to up their work rate we ask them to rate themselves on a scale of one to ten on how hard they have worked during the game. We then help them come up with three things they could do in the next training session or game that would increase this number. They then review this target each time they play until they can rate themselves honestly at a ten.'

A good coach can help with this process too. It's obvious to say that if a coach can let a player know what they can do to raise their performance in a specific area, then a player can try to do this. Unfortunately, we find that not every player is fortunate enough to play for coaches like David and his colleagues at Liverpool.

His thoughts on reflection and setting personal aims also hold true. 'We've worked with players who keep "learning logs" where they write their thoughts on their performance and what the manager has said to them and consistently learn from them. Players like this just get better and better through into their late thirties. We also know players who were getting tips on how to improve their game at 16, yet are still making the same mistakes when they retire.'

The education of coaches in the psychological areas of the game is something else that David is passionate about. 'There is an increase in the number of psychology courses that coaches can go on, but many of them focus on theoretical concepts. What we need to do more of is learn from the best. For example, Jose Mourinho clearly has a talent for "togetherness" in a team. If we want to develop, the coaches of the future need to know the strategies that he uses.

'There is something even more important than all of this at academy level. The mental performance skills, such as developing confidence, control, and the ability to relax, learn and plan for the future, are skills that players need for life. We've got to be mindful that some research highlights that only about 3 per cent of players who play youth football for professional clubs will still be playing professional football at the age of 23. This is a pretty stark statistic, but it underlines the need for players to develop these skills.'

'If you don't set goals for yourself, you are doomed to work to achieve the goals of someone else.' Brian Tracy, international speaker, consultant and author

APPENDICES

YOUR SEVEN-DAY CHALLENGE

For the tools and techniques in this book to be most effective they must become a habit. In order for them to become a habit, you must build a routine.

We have developed the seven-day challenge below as a way of building the mental strategies you need to make the very most of your potential. We suggest following it as closely as possible at first, allowing of course for any midweek games or fixture changes, until the activities become a habit.

Details of all these activities can be found in this book.

TABLE APP.1 THE SEVEN-DAY CHALLENGE

Day	Activity
Day 1	Create your future history for the week ahead Five minutes mental rehearsal of the day ahead Create a playlist of relaxing music for your MP3 player
Day 2	Five minutes of visualisation Set mini aims for today's training Review future history Create anchor for confidence or some other useful state

Day	Activity
Day 3	Five minutes of visualisation Work out your 'anger' strategy and how to stop it Attempt breathing focus exercise
Day 4	Five minutes of visualisation Do breathing focus exercise until you get to 100 Create trigger phrases to use to refocus during games
Day 5	Five minutes of visualisation Review future history created at the beginning of the week Set mini aims for training Later in the day, use relaxation music along with breathing technique for twenty minutes' relaxation Choose ideal states for match day
Day 6	(match day) Five minutes of visualisation Set match aims Use specific tools and techniques to create appropriate states in the lead-up to the game Use trigger phrases to keep focused during the game
Day 7	Five minutes of visualisation Mental review of only things that went well in the game

Start the process again on day eight.

ADDITIONAL READING AND RESOURCES

Books

In Pursuit of Excellence by Terry Orlick (Human Kinetics, 2007)
A good place to start if you are interested in the theory behind some elements of this book.

The Mental Edge: Maximize Your Sports Potential with the Mind-body Connection by Kenneth Baum (Perigree, 1999)
Another perspective on mental development in sport, with a greater focus on the body and mind.

Mind Games: Inspirational Lessons from the World's Finest Sports Stars by Jeff Grout and Sarah Perrin (Capstone, 2006)
If you have enjoyed the case studies and anecdotal stories in this book, you will enjoy *Mind Games*. It is full of comments from interviews with professional athletes.

The Complete Guide To Sports Motivation by Ken Hodge (A&C Black, 2005)
Another book with some great tools and techniques to draw from.

Be Happy Now (Hay House, 2007); *You Can Have What You Want* by Michael Neill (Hay House, 2006)
Both books help you to do exactly what the titles suggest. Although they are written for anybody to improve their lives, they are full of tools that you can apply to improve your game.

The Art of Possibility by Benjamin and Rosamund Zander (Penguin, 2006)
An unusual but easy read with tales from a range of backgrounds to help you enjoy life more.

Tools for Engagement by Eric Jensen (Corwin Press, 2003)
Our favourite work on states and state management. Combines theory and practical tools brilliantly.

Notes from a Friend by Anthony Robbins (Pocket Books, 2001)
One of the original books from the world's best-known success coach.

The Secret by Rhonda Byrne (Simon & Schuster, 2006)
A best-seller that goes way beyond the tools covered in this book. If you want a totally alternative view on how to get what you want in life, try this.

The Leadership Challenge 4th ed. by James Kouzes and Barry Posner (Jossey Bass, 2007)
Still the best work on leadership we've ever come across.

The Learning Brain by Eric Jensen and Gary Johnson (Brain Store Inc, 1994)
Another book from one of our favourite authors on learning and the brain.

You Can't Afford the Luxury of a Negative Thought by John-Roger and Peter McWilliams (Thorsons, 2001)
Another view on the power of thought and how to take control of your own mind.

The Trust Effect by Larry Reynolds (Nicholas Brealey, 1997)
In our experience, football is one of the lowest trust industries around. Even applying one or two tools from this powerful book will make a huge difference in some clubs.

The Solutions Focus by Mark McKergow and Paul Z. Jackson (Nicholas Brealey, 2006)
A brilliant book! A simple approach to focusing on solutions in order to get better results.

Films to watch

Any Given Sunday – Includes one of the most powerful half-time talks ever heard. We know of several professional managers who have used this speech to lift their players.

Coach Carter – A fantastic tale, based on a true story of a high-school coach who brings together a basketball team in the toughest of circumstances.

Useful websites

www.successinfootball.com
www.kaizen-training.com
www.thefa.com
www.geniuscatalyst.com
www.ukfootballcoachingnetwork.co.uk
www.beswickssports.com
www.acblack.com